A
GOOD
TALK

A

GOOD

TALK

THE STORY AND SKILL

OF CONVERSATION

DANIEL MENAKER

NEW YORK · TWELVE · BOSTON

Twelve
Hachette Book Group
237 Park Avenue
New York, NY 10017

www.HachetteBookGroup.com

Twelve is an imprint of Grand Central Publishing.
The Twelve name and logo are trademarks of Hachette Book Group, Inc.

Book design by Fearn Cutler de Vicq

Printed in the United States of America

First Edition: January 2010
10 9 8 7 6 5 4 3 2

Grateful acknowledgments are made to Xavier Dufail for permission to
reprint the picture of the chimpanzees; and to Rockmasters International
Network, INC. for permission to quote from "If You Want to Be Happy."

Library of Congress Cataloging-in-Publication Data
Menaker, Daniel.
   A good talk : the story and skill of conversation / Daniel Menaker. — 1st ed.
   p. cm.
   Includes bibliographical references.
   Summary: "A stylish, funny and surprising guide to the art of
converstation"—Provided by the publisher.
ISBN 978-0-446-54002-5 (alk. paper)
1. Conversation analysis. I. Title.
P95.45.M46 2010
302.3'46—dc22   2009013143

For William and Elizabeth

CONTENTS

CHAPTER ONE

OPENING REMARKS

⬩⬩⬩

In this book I want to talk about the story and shapes and skills of conversation and also, ultimately, about conversations, no matter how transient they may be, as a kind of artifact—a human art of great importance produced by all people everywhere. But let's start at the beginning. We can be certain that this exclusively human activity called conversation didn't start out particularly shaped or aesthetical. No one can know how language began, but that hasn't stopped anyone from speculating about the matter.

I've always guessed that human language had to begin

with grunts that developed into one or both kinds of pragmatically crucial "first" speech. One is naming or calling out of names—at the outset, of individual or groups of human beings, especially when they were out of visual range, as they might be in a hunting party; then of objects and animals and places and the weather. Something equivalent to our "John" must have been an early proper noun. Same with "Mary," "gazelle!" "hot!" "cave," "lion!" "not tonight," and "headache."

My other speculation about first speech is that it was orders or directions. Very close to naming. Let's say that the prehistoric equivalent of Mary had a daughter who would probably today be named Meghan. Let's say Mary was weaving a thatch of reeds for the roof of their hovel. Meghan, ten years old now and irritable about the fact that virtually nothing—from jump rope to television—had been invented, was mooning and sighing around the hovel with nothing to do. Mary needed more reeds, a stack of which her John had piled up outside the hovel, so she grabbed Meghan's arm and pointed toward the reeds and uttered something that eventually came to mean more or less "Fetch!" There followed a rash of people using this order all the time, until someone came up with the words "Oh, Mom!" and, probably later, "Get it yourself."

By the way, there is a word for the study of the origin of language: glottogony. It turns out that a lot of academics subscribe, roughly, to the naming/orders glottological theory that has always seemed to me to make sense. Biologists, evolutionary and otherwise, have made their own contributions to the understanding of the development of language by demonstrating that somewhere between a hundred thousand and fifty thousand years ago, the human larynx migrated, through mutation and natural selection, in such a way as to facilitate speech, perhaps as a result of *Homo* going *erectus* on the savannas and veldts. (A short-story submission I once read took place on what the author referred to as "the African svelte"—which, it now suddenly occurs to me, may be an accidental portmanteau of "savanna" and "veld.") It descended a little and assumed an L shape. The larynx, I mean.

There also appears to have been at around the same time—the time of hominids leaving the jungle for the plains—another crucial mutation in a certain gene, the FOXP2 gene (shown here so that you can recognize it whenever the need arises)—

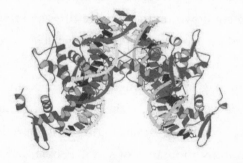

which led to the development of Broca's and Wernicke's areas (just south of the amygdala, off Exit 19). This important advance in the evolution of the human brain helped to facilitate speech. And it happened to *all* of them before the hominids left Africa, perhaps starting with Mitochondrial Eve, the mother who began all others. The mutation spread quickly because it was so helpful to hunting and gathering and was thus a natural selection for natural selection. That's why when the species spread out from Africa, it developed languages wherever it went.

One of the ways that scientists got onto this gene's role in language was the discovery not long ago that four generations of a modern family that had certain severe troubles in talking had a new, *bad* mutation at FOXP2. When you put all this and some other factors together—my guesswork, fossil evidence (of larynx bones), the deforestation of hominids, the FOXP2 gene, the need for foragers to go out on the svelte and come back with good directions to where the doomed antelope were playing that day, the use of tools, which required early man except the Jews and the Italians to cut down on the hand gestures and ramp up the larynx, and the real advantages of being able to communicate in the dark ("Faster!")—you get: language.

But language is not conversation, and conversation is what we are here to discuss, one of these days. It apparently could have been the case that language and speech preceded conversation by thousands of years. People, or something like them, may well have gone around just naming things for quite a while, expressing anger and ordering others around—you can still hear traces of this proto-language in New York City traffic jams—and conveying important information, such as "A saber-toothed tiger is coming" or "A little of this stuff that I herewith name 'garlic' improves the taste of antelope meat" or "The crushed and macerated leaves of that plant will help your acne." Those may be fine things to say, but they aren't conversation. Conversation started, I think, when, for example, to the first sentence a hearer responded, "I just want to tell you how much I've appreciated your help through the years, John," or to the second, "How did you discover that?" or to the third, "Great! The prom is this Saturday night."

That is, conversation can certainly contain and almost always does contain pragmatic information and pure expressions of emotion and so on, but for me, to be *real* conversation, it also has to include thoughts and ideas and reactions that are not simply reflexive and that have no immediate practical use. If it is all immediate usefulness, then we call it trigonometry class or a conference call or *This Old House*. (Not those useless but evidently still necessary primate rituals called business meetings, however—meetings are generally not much good for anything. Samuel Johnson once said that conversation is what's left when business is done.) So, then, let's take speech and language as givens, because they are. I mean, we all have them, even deaf people, whose sign language fits the definition of language in every way, unless you require audibility. I just thought that because we can't have conversations without them, it would be a good idea to give them a nod at the start. But now: How and why did the activity we call conversation begin?

One way to attempt to answer the question is to work backward from what conversations generally consist of to how they may have originated, and that is exactly what Professor Robin Dunbar (among others), of the University of Liverpool, has done in his book *Grooming, Gossip, and the Evolution of Language.* Dunbar postulates that conversation, especially gossip, began as a hands-free substitute for physical grooming,

as hands were beginning to come in so . . . handy for other, newfangled purposes: tool making, sewing and reaping, cooking, cave painting. You could get real practical opposable-thumb things done *and,* at the same time, point out that the gigantic glacier seemed to be getting closer every day or that this new, very hot "fire" thing seemed extremely interesting. Now, when I say "gossip," you may not think of gossip as a real and respectable form of conversation, but you'd better. According to another social psychologist, Nicholas Emler, of the London School of Economics, more than 80 percent of our talk is about other specific and named individuals—in other words, gossip, or something very close to it. This leaves less than 20 percent for the meaning of life and cosmology and whether Cézanne's work anticipated scientific discoveries about the neurology of vision. (It did.) And many scholars have established that gossip gives us a way to examine ourselves and others with regard to in-bounds and out-of-bounds social behavior. So it is not only respectable and universal but also essential. And fun.

Here is a bit of gossip I shouldn't but will tell you. A colleague of mine once asked me as we were walking back to work after lunch if I would give him a recommendation for a job he was applying for at another company. I said that I was sort of under an obligation to act in the best interests of the company that employed both of us, and that he had already put me in a somewhat difficult position. He asked again, more insistently, as he was very unhappy in his current work situation. I told him that I really didn't think we should discuss the matter any further. He left the company shortly after that but not for the job he wanted. Later, I talked the situation over with a close friend, who ended up berating me for not helping the guy out. He said that I had been too rigid in following "the company line." I replied that at least I had kept the other guy's wish to leave a secret. "Shouldn't that count for something?" I asked. My friend said, "A little. Maybe." Now, do you see how many social norms these two instances of gossip involved? I sort of do, in fact. In any case, the received wisdom about gossip is that it serves a social-policing function.

Professor Dunbar also theorizes that the size of animals' social groups, especially primates' social groups, corresponds directly to the size of their neocortexes. In humans, our neocortex dictates that we can maintain social ties with about a hundred and fifty people per person. Chimps generally hang out with some fifty other chimps. Just think of us rushing frantically from dwelling to dwelling or Starbucks to Starbucks trying to comb the hair of our hundred and fifty closest friends. We would surely all have to have buzz cuts; without one, a person like this girl I knew once, whom I'll call Tawnee, would require for her astounding thick hair about three delightful hours all by herself. But, Dunbar says, precisely because we can't possibly manually delouse all those people—chimps spend 20 percent of their time combing and inspecting one another—we developed conversation. You can converse with four or five people at the same time, and you can also, if need be, simultaneously sharpen arrowheads, cement the stones of a castle keep, or drive a car, depending on your era.

However it came about neurologically and evolutionarily, communicating with one another for no immediate reason has to be the most quintessentially and exclusively human of all our behaviors. According to Emler, the average person of our time spends about 80 percent of his or her life in the company of other people and between six and twelve hours every day talking to those other people. He has also found that self-disclosure accounts for two-thirds of those six to twelve hours, and he breaks down *that* large symphony of talk into smaller melodies: about 10 percent for states of mind ("I fear Greeks, even when they bear gifts"—Virgil, *The Aeneid*) or body ("My head is bloody, but unbow'd"—William Ernest Henley, "Invictus") and allotments for preferences, plans, and, the largest of all in this self-disclosure catalog, what Michael Gazzaniga, the neuroscientist and author of *Human*, calls "doings" ("I found my thrill / On Blueberry Hill"—Fats Domino, "Blueberry Hill"). That is, narrative. That is, storytelling. Finally, in this conversation quantification derby, back to Professor Dunbar, who tells us, in *Grooming, Gossip, and the Evolution of Language,* that men and women speak about an equal amount—could you have fooled me, or what?—but that men spend two out of every three of their conversational minutes talking about themselves, whereas women spend only about a third of the time doing so.

That makes for an exemplary pie chart, maybe, but it and many other of the conversational data seem suspect to me. For example, assuming that what passes for arithmetic in my brain is right, if two-thirds of everyone's conversation consists of self-disclosure, how can it be that women talk about themselves only a third of the time? Or something like that. More puzzling still is the certitude with which these researchers appear to have decided what qualifies as talking about oneself vs. talking about others. Take the example Gazzaniga cites of a woman—a woman on the catty side, perhaps—who, he says, is talking about someone else: "'And the last time I saw her, I swear she had gained twenty-five pounds.'" Is that person really talking about the other person? Doesn't her proclivity for such observations, assuming that she has such a proclivity, say more about herself than it does about the weight gainer? Isn't everything we say—at least beyond "Turn right," "What's up?" and "Next!"—self-disclosing? I think so. As Agatha Christie said, "There is nothing so dangerous for anyone who has something to hide as conversation! A human being . . . cannot resist the opportunity to reveal himself and express his personality which conversation gives him. Every time he will give himself away."

This particular kind of question is particularly important! Because it indicates the complicated and enmeshing nature of good conversation—the lovely pot-holder-esque undistentangleability of it. And those qualities are what often make conversations so gratifying, I think, and what also make them a kind of art. Some are simple and basic, like a child's finger painting. Some have more texture, like a proficient still life. And many are rich and complex, like a Vermeer. Like art, they all have in common the absence of direct *utility*. Some parts of a conversation usually do have some immediate application, and, as I hope to convince you, conversations definitely have noble benefits that transcend the merely pragmatic. But their most important apparent ingredient—one produced by curiosity, reverie, humor, and playfully associational thinking—is *aimlessness*, in that word's most neutral definition. Maybe I should write it this way: aim-less-ness. In his engrossing book *Conversation: A History of a Declining Art*, Stephen Miller gives conversation a similar (if in my view slightly too negative) definition: "Talk without purpose." It may be aimless, but it's not purposeless, as Professor Dunbar has tried to demonstrate evolutionarily and as I hope to show presently.

In an acquisitions meeting at a publishing company whose identity I'll disguise by calling it Camouflage Books, my colleagues and I were discussing how much to offer for a book proposal that claimed to shed new light on the assassination of John F. let's say Shmennedy. One of the people at the meeting (guess who) said about Lee Harvey Shmoswald's hiding place, "You know, I've always been curious about what a 'book depository' actually *is*." Another person—an excellent firecracker of a publisher with a no-nonsense demeanor—said, "Well, why don't you just hold a seminar on that subject after working hours, Shman? Right now we're trying to figure out what to bid on this project." Shman must have thought, Ouch! No aim-less-ness in stock there. And therefore no conversation, either.

That episode dramatizes the seemingly inevitable conflict between conversation and almost all forms of "results"-oriented human discourse. It's this antagonism—especially in our hyped-up, sound-bite-ridden, profit-hungry global culture—that Stephen Miller and many sociologists hold responsible for the reduction in time we spend conversing. (And reading.) Especially, as Miller laments, in the United States, which, with its pioneering and commercial-traveling and river-damming and belching-smokestack and generally intensely pragmatic and often John Wayne–like ethos and history, has always cast a more critical eye on aim-less social intercourse than have many other modern societies.

Speaking of history—as I will try to do, briefly and with some futility, in the next chapter of this book—since the 1960s, starting with the work of Harvey Sacks, we have in modern times formalized the study of conversation in a sociological discipline called "conversation analysis." That the practitioners and observers of this discipline have abbreviated it to "CA" speaks V's to me about its generally dry tone. Here are some books and articles you can consult to see if I'm right:

Structures of Social Action: Studies in Conversation Analysis
Garfinkel and Ethnomethodology
"Phonetic Detail and the Organisation of Talk-in-Interaction"
Doing Phonology
"Agreeing and Disagreeing with Assessment: Some Features of Preferred/Dispreferred Turn Shapes"
Sequence Organization in Interaction: A Primer in Conversation Analyis, Volume 1

Pretty daunting—though I like the sound of *Doing Phonology*. I've always had a weakness for the gerundive titles of yesteryear—*Raising Arizona, Letting Go, Saving Private Ryan, Driving Miss Daisy,* "(Sittin' on) The Dock of the Bay." In many examples of CA you will find discussions not only of turn-constructional units (TCUs; I'm not kidding), but of turn allocational components, sequence organization, adjacency pairs, and preference organization.

Other terms refer not only to mumbling and misspeaking, but to gaffes—who fixes them and how. Gaffes can destroy a conversation more violently than anything else. I have a very good friend who has a large red Gorbachev-class birthmark on her cheek—it's very noticeable. She visited me in the country once, and the first morning, while she was sitting at the dining room table and I was holding a frying pan and serving her bacon that was still sizzling, I said to her, "Lean back a little or you might be permanently disfigured." The discipline of conversational analysis often uses the term "repair organization" for times when conversations break down and are restarted. The repair organization must have been on a break that morning of the bacon.

We can chuckle at the reconditeness of its terms, but CA has sometimes proven helpful to understanding and even improving some important kinds of conversations—like those between doctors and patients, journalists and their subjects, attorneys and witnesses in court, and family members. It has even been applied with some interesting results to the Nixon White House tapes, or so I've read. The tapes usually involve language so opaque that you might think the participants were deliberately disguising their meanings in some weird code:

H. R. "BOB" HALDEMAN: We had [Charles "Chuck"]
    Colson make a . . .

PRESIDENT NIXON: Chuck is something else.

HALDEMAN: Yeah. You know, [Edmund] Muskie sent
    those oranges down to the veterans—that group
    on Saturday, I mean.

PRESIDENT NIXON: Yeah.

HALDEMAN: He didn't go down himself, but he sent
    oranges.

PRESIDENT NIXON: Did Colson order some oranges for
    him?

HALDEMAN: Colson sent oranges out yesterday. [*laughs*]
    From Muskie.

PRESIDENT NIXON: Is it out?

HALDEMAN: I don't know whether it's out yet or not.
    They'll get it out. [*laughs*]

PRESIDENT NIXON: He just ordered them?

HALDEMAN: [*laughs*] Yeah. An awful lot of cases of
    oranges. I don't know how the hell he does that
    stuff, but he . . . It's good, you know, he's been
    around the District here so long, he has a lot of
    contacts, and he, as a local guy, he can get stuff
    done here that . . . And he's got no— He's going
    to get caught in some of those things [*unclear*].

PRESIDENT NIXON: [*unclear*] Well, he has been caught.

HALDEMAN: [*unclear*] And he has been caught.

PRESIDENT NIXON: It's all right.

Medical or political, even in raw transcripts of basically
banal exchanges there have to be many layers of unspoken
subtext. My point is that like works of art, and most human
transactions, anything more than truly rudimentary talk
("Have some?" "Yes, please") has innumerable nuances,
including what the observer himself brings to it—a sketchy
knowledge of the language being spoken, for example, or
being heartbroken, or in love, or sleepy, or drunk. Even
video recordings of a conversation, which can of course

show some body language, can't reproduce the event's entirety. None of the subjects' pheromones waft through the air, the people look five to ten pounds heavier than they are, the colors aren't true. And, as is the case with our real-life experience, no amount of transcription, recording, or even being present—or even MRIs—can tell us with any precision what is going on in another person's mind. Or in our own, really, for that matter. And these latencies are surely important ingredients of any conversation.

So maybe the best way to understand what's going on when we talk to one another, and to get better at it and enjoy it more, is to approach this exclusively human activity the way a good critic approaches any other human artifact that has inexhaustibly various aspects. That's part of what I'll do here, in the hope that it will interest, entertain, and benefit readers—partners in the conversation that any writer is implicitly having with them, even if those readers can answer only silently. After a brief look at the history of conversation, I'll address its components through an examination of a single specific recorded conversation, held over a meal between me and someone I know only slightly. I paid for the meal. Actually, I paid for *five* meals, four of them not with me as a participant, but one of the first recorded conversers pulled out of the deal later on because he thought he had divulged too much—especially about one of his wife's obstetricians. I'll discuss better and worse ways to think about and approach these conversational components and try to show that there is a "deep structure" that underlies many conversations. The main focus here will be on those situations in which we talk for an hour or so to someone we don't know very well or at all—at a party, on an airplane (*two very clearly consenting participants required!*), at a bar, and on many other kinds of occasions, both planned and unplanned. My partner in this conversation and I are both writers, but there were many differences between us as well—age, gender, background, religion, and so on. And I believe that the way our talk went is, however loosely, the way most spontaneous talks go, barring extreme disparities in the personal circumstances—wealth, poverty, mental illness, and so on—of the talkers. (By the way, I think airplane passengers should all be asked to wear something like Indian caste marks on their foreheads—red for "No talking, please," green for "Yes, you can tell me about your cousin's goiter, and I will tell you about Tawnee, who broke my heart." Or little face icons, maybe, with zipped or unzipped lips. I've been passionate about the issue of airplane conversations ever since I more or less conquered my fear of flying and too soon afterward sat next to a woman who for more than two hours told me why she was so afraid of flying.)

The underlying conversational structure I've mentioned consists—shockingly, I realize—of a beginning, middle, and end. But, as I hope chapters 3 and 4 will show (two chapters only because one would be too long), it's more topic-specific and interesting than that. Greetings are sometimes fraught: After all, the handshake grew out of the custom of demonstrating that one isn't carrying a concealed weapon. Fraught example: A fairly good young friend recently came to my house for dinner and noticed that I was wearing a (very manly!) bracelet—a recent addition to my possessions, much less expensive than your usual late-middle-age, jaunty-sports-car-convertible, death-denying protest vehicle. "What's that, Dan?" he said as we showed each other that we didn't have concealed weapons. "It's a bracelet," I said. "I thought it was a watch at first," he said with disappointment. "No, it's a bracelet," I said. "Well," he said, without a trace of humor or irony or any other hint of mitigation, "it makes you look like a fag." So it might be interesting and helpful to take a closer look at the way hellos work.

The main part of a conversation, particularly with a new acquaintance, establishes some kind of common ground. In the rare event that it doesn't, the whole meeting will be something of a failure. Finding that common ground and then moving beyond often has two stages. The first is the Survey, in which the people involved discuss some important aspects of their identities. The second stage is Discovery, in which sometimes significant connections are unearthed: "We have the same middle names!" "My kids don't get along very well, either." These, again, can be trivial or revealing: "I have flat feet," "I had a one-night stand two days before I got married—two days minus one day, to be completely honest." This second phase often increases the sense of trust between the two conversants, and that trust in turn leads them to take Risks.

Finally, as a conversation develops, the two people occasionally and often sporadically take on defined Roles, particularly when there are large age or status or other differences between them: confessor and confessee, adviser and advisee, pursuer and pursuee, hothead and cool cucumber, comic and straight man, new kid and old hand, and so on. It's as if they are improvising a play about themselves. This spontaneous scripting usually comes in waves, which then recede, leaving renewed spontaneity in their place.

When you turn off the engines of some old cars, they go on chugging for a while—a phenomenon called "dieseling." Trying to conclude a conversation often has the same result—it can sputter away for minutes on end, longer than any of its participants want it to. I'm going to battle against talking about the dialogic differences between men and women, but sometimes I'm going to lose. Like right now: Women take longer to say good-bye than men do, and to see the certainty I have on this subject, however anecdotal that certainty may be, say out loud the name of the punctuation mark at the end of this sentence.

In any case, generally, and for similarly primal reasons, the end of a conversation can be as awkward as its beginning—the Beatles made a whole song out of the confusion and complexity that attend "good-bye." I believe that like the terminal part of everything of any importance—war, sex, movies, life, chess games, books, entire civilizations, hot-fudge sundaes, and chapters 3 and 4 themselves—the end of a conversation repays some attention.

"You have to write about telephone conversations." "I hope you're going to discuss what people should do when others repeat themselves." "What about job interviews?" "What should people talk about on a first date?" "I wish you would tell how to handle insults or remarks that are offensive in other ways." "Bores! What do you do about them? How do you know if you're one of them?" "Will you talk about people who repeat themselves all the time?" "How do you handle it if you can't remember someone's name?" "What about people who don't listen because they're always trying to think of what they want to say next?" "Should you tell people when they say the same things over and over again?" "Is IM'ing conversation?" "What about race, religion, politics?" People would sometimes come close to *shouting* such topics at me when I first mentioned the idea of this book, so chapter 5 will be a sort of FAQ (frequently arising quandaries) miscellany that addresses some of the conversational issues the yellers yelled at me to include. It was partly such vehement urgings, which mainly took the form of peeves, that convinced me, when I first began to talk about it, that such a project might find an interested audience. My qualifications to weigh in even lightly on such questions consist mainly of fifty years' worth of the kinds of normal personal exchanges we all have and forty-five years' worth of supernumerous, highly social, and often fraught professional exchanges, during too many of which I have wandered or blundered into deep trouble, stepping on others' toes, having mine stepped on, or stepping on my own.

Distilling an approach to conversation based on the meeting of the two sample talkers of chapters 3 and 4 and the peeve-remedial efforts of chapter 5, the next chapter will rip your head half-off with its insight, drama, vampires, political skulduggery, and wet-T-shirt-vs.-Chippendale's photo-essay. No, really, that last clause contains (I hope) molecules of the three qualities of a good conversationalist that I have found essential: curiosity, humor, and impudence. And they will, just a *little* less excitingly, be the real subject of chapter 6.

Sometimes the richest and most satisfying rewards of talking to others come to you later, in solitude, if you know how to look back at them. You realize that someone was flirting with you. You realize that you were flirting with him. Or you sense that your companion may be thinking about offering you a job. Perhaps you understand that you were both basically discussing regrets and giving reassurance to each other. That is, generally you understand that despite the seeming aimlessness of the chat, themes and even deep concerns permeated it. If you're lucky, you'll also feel some of the psychologically and even physiologically beneficial effects that talking to others brings with it. That very important and not widely understood retrospective component of conversation will be taken up in chapter 7, along with some reflections on conversation's social, political, and moral dimensions—the kind of reflection that usually has no place in conversations themselves but that I hope will contribute at least a little to an understanding of the crucial role they may now more than ever play in overcoming a new, global world's bitter divisions.

Very pleased to meet you.

CHAPTER TWO

TALKING HISTORY

In an exciting and shall we say colorful conversation I once had with the fire-breathing best-selling author of books that question some of our most basic intellectual assumptions, he said of historians, "They're all frauds. They know what happened and they can make any shape they want to out of it." I have been thinking about this idea ever since, and have come to believe it, in a way, more and more strongly. Not that historians cannot be brilliant and helpful in finding facts and trying to bring order to the radical chaos of the past, but their constructions and interpretations of events—especially their casual explanations—are almost by definition questionable. The very *pastness* of the past—particularly complex developments—renders historical theories un-provable, it seems to me. And historians' own views of life must necessarily color their views of history.

Who is to say that because James Boswell set down in no doubt sanitized writing many of Samuel Johnson's pronouncements and we happen to know about them, they are of greater conversational originality or interest or insight than what two old Maori friends said to each other in the thirteenth century while fishing off the coast near what is now Auckland? Not me. If scholars can't agree on the causes of World War I or the proportion of idealism to commerce in the motives for the American Revolution, how can anyone present a history of so literally airy a subject as conversation? Even a tentative one?

And then there's this: The first known recording of a human voice was made in 1860, seventeen years before Edison turns out *not* to have made history by recording himself reciting "Mary Had a Little Lamb." It was the French who got there first, of course—that nation of salon *gomme-flappiers*. To be exact, it was a Parisian inventor named Édouard-Léon Scott de Martinville, who used something called a phonoautograph to inscribe sound waves of a woman, probably his daughter, singing "Au Claire de la Lune" onto paper covered with the soot from an oil lamp. If Edison had had a daughter, he'd have done well to get her to recite "Mary Had a Little Lamb," because even allowing for the primitive nature of the equipment he was using, he sounds close to tubercular.

The point is that for conversations, we have nothing that even resembles what historians call "primary sources"—contemporary documents, photographs, and the like—from before the time of Monsieur Scott de Martinville's *fille*. With movies we have movies. With the Declaration of Independence, we have the Declaration of Independence, not the Declaration of Independence as Recalled to the Best of His Ability by Button Gwinnet. With a driver who ran the light at a major intersection in Des Moines, we have a surveillance camera digital recording, not just a cop trying to fill that month's ticket quota. The idea of primary sources itself is controversial, but whatever they are or aren't, it's safe to say that we have had nothing really close to them for conversation—that is, people having conversations—until quite recently. To make the matter even more confusing, we don't even know what we don't know. As you'll soon see, if you hadn't already realized it, many scholars put Socrates at the head of the list of conversational giants, chronologically and in other ways. But we don't know at all that Socrates didn't learn all his gigantic tricks from Shmocrates, a modest teacher who lived just the other side of the Parthenon.

Still, the Western canon insists on being fired when any cultural subject is within its range, and conversation is a fair target, even given all the epistemological bafflements I've just described. While I load it up, just a couple of over-arching considerations:

1. Conversation as I've defined it—essentially "aim-less" social talk—might sometimes seem to be a luxury born of prosperity and leisure, no matter how minimal. And it's true that under some circumstances and at some extremes, talking can be an indulgence, even a decadent one. But when there's no food to eat, it turns out that conversation basically disappears. Those horrific refugee camps in North Africa, of which we continue to see so many species-shaming pictures, where victims of tribal violence foregather to starve to death, are almost entirely silent, save for the sounds of suffering and the buzzing of flies, when television cameras drop by to record their misery. But given what all the anthropologists and other researchers consider to be the non-self-indulgent nature of conversation— our race's *necessity* for it—its absence under such dire conditions is actually just another example of the privations of extreme poverty.

2. The epochally important conversationalists whom you're about to meet are to this subject what Captain Ahab is to fishing. I mean, they may be

famous, they may have set a style for some others, their voices (or at least the idea of their voices) may still be ringing in our ears. But it is you and I and other ordinary people who create the history of conversation, insofar as there is one. Two examples: The casual use of obscenities has gone up a shitload in the last decade or so, not because Nixon cursed so much in the White House, but because for some (to me) lamentable reason, you and I have allowed it. Or even participated in it. Or encouraged it. *That's* an example of the history of conversation. Similarly, in the United States, use of the honorifics "Mister," "Miss," "Mrs.," and "Ms." has diminished tremendously over the last half century—a result, I believe, of the phonier aspects of American congeniality and informality, and a literal product of unrestrained corporate greed, with its cozying up to the consumer, and of crossbreeding with the legacy of American egalitarianism. After all, "Mister" is a variant of "Master," "Miss" and "Mrs." of "Mistress," and "Ms." is a similarly deferential variant thereof; and we are the only nation that will not dip its flag in ceremonial deference at the opening ceremonies of the Olympics.

Deferential courtesies have always gone against the American grain, to some extent, and now that extent is nearly complete. It's part of the same mentality that prompted George Bush and now almost every other politician to substitute "folks" for "people" whenever possible—including even, and ridiculously, "There are folks out there who are trying to kill us." We are now a nation not of first-meeting Misters and Misses, but of folks—of Harolds and Kumars, of Bobs and Teds and Carols and Alices, of Phils and Dons, of Kathie Lees and Regises. It seems to me a shame in both cases, not because language should be clean or we should be formal, but because making cursing commonplace and abandoning honorifics reduce the range of expression and inflection we can use in conversation.

If you meet someone under somewhat formal circumstances and she calls you Mr. Smith and you call her Ms. Jones, it means that after you've established some mutual congeniality, you can invite more informality by saying, "Please call me Will," and, "Please call me Norah." If it's Will and Norah from the start, this friendly device is disabled. I was once introduced to Bernard Malamud in the offices of *The New Yorker,* because I was going to apprentice-edit a story of his, and we shook hands and he said, "Good to meet you, Mr. Menaker," and I said, "Call me Dan, please," and he said, "So soon?" (As long as I'm dropping names, I met Isaac Bashevis Singer under exactly the same circumstances a little later and, having learned my old-world manners lesson from Mr. Malamud, said, "It's good to meet you, Mr. Singer." To which, after looking me up and down, Mr. Singer replied with similar Yiddish-style conciseness, "So young?")

As far as *!()& cursing is concerned, where the *!()& do you go for the *!()& language of <u>real</u> *!()& anger or genuinely transgressive *!()& obscenities when you *!()& spend all of the words in obscenity's wallet on cheap, everyday, nondescript communication? This is a lost battle and a lost conversational resource.

The annals of Western conversation generally start with Socrates, and here he is at last, emerging from the baths in Athens with nothing on but sandals. But talk about no primary sources! We have at best second- and thirdhand accounts not only of his appearance, but of his demeanor, his habits, his personal life, his words, his ideas, and, most important for our purposes, his conversation. Not a single word from his own stylus and no contemporary likenesses.

We are told that Socrates' outward appearance was crude and his face grotesque. He had a thick neck, a front portico, and his eyes popped out a little. He had a pug nose with wide nostrils, a large mouth, and coarse lips.

But among many Athenians he held a place of high esteem because of his military valor and his philosophical genius. Young people in particular admired him. Much of what we know of him comes to us by way of Xenophon—the contemporary soldier/military historian/quasi-philosopher and expert on horse bits—and Plato, Socrates' student, admirer, and amanuensis. Many scholars believe that in his later writings, Plato used him as a dummy, a sort of classical Greek Socrates puppet, through whom he broadcast his own theories. Some researchers have gone so far as to suggest that Socrates didn't exist at all, but there seem to be enough crumbs of contemporary allusion and historical record to establish with something close to certainty that he did.

What Socrates is often said to have done for conversation was this: By asking a series of seemingly simple but actually fiendishly leading questions, he challenged received political, moral, and philosophical wisdom. His wife, Xanthippe, was much younger than he was, and a shrew.

"Xanthippe" is now sometimes used as a generic name for her kind of character—as are for other qualities the names of Jesus, Napoleon, Cassandra, and Mickey Mouse. Perhaps because she was such a . . . such a . . . Xanthippe! at home, Socrates wandered about Athens, particularly its marketplace, the *agora*, practicing *elenchus* (meaning either "scrutiny" or "refutation," depending on who is doing the translating), which he used in a series of questions that led to a revision or subversion of various pieties and platitudes. For example, from the *Apology*—Plato's account of Socrates' trial—in which the main spokesman for the accusers was a young man with a bad beard named Meletus:

Come hither, Meletus, and let me ask a question of you. You think a great deal about the improvement of youth?

Yes, I do.

Tell the judges, then, who is their improver; for you must know, as you have taken the pains to discover their corrupter, and are citing and accusing me before them. Speak, then, and tell the judges who their improver is. Observe, Meletus, that you are silent, and have nothing to say. But is not this rather disgraceful, and a very considerable proof of what I was saying, that you have no interest in the matter? Speak up, friend, and tell us who their improver is.

The laws.

But that, my good sir, is not my meaning. I want to know who the person is, who, in the first place, knows the laws.

The judges, Socrates, who are present in court.

What do you mean to say, Meletus, that they are able to instruct and improve youth?

Certainly they are.

What, all of them, or some only and not others?

All of them.

By the goddess Hera, that is good news! There are plenty of improvers, then. And what do you say of the audience—do they improve them?

Yes, they do.

And the senators?

Yes, the senators improve them.

But perhaps the members of the citizen assembly corrupt them?—or do they too improve them?

They improve them.

Then every Athenian improves and elevates them; all with the exception of myself; and I alone am their corrupter? Is that what you affirm?

Perhaps most famously of all, besides welcoming with astonishing equanimity his death-by-hemlock sentence (for "corrupting" the youth of Athens and substituting his own gods for the city's), Socrates demonstrated the ignorance of the allegedly wise. Many consider his probing interrogations to be the basis of the scientific method, which requires starting one's intellectual journey with an admission of *not* knowing in order to reach the destination of knowing. Similarly, as many philosophers themselves have said, much if not all of Western philosophy appears to have started here. Socrates, possibly for the first time, used the process of the relentlessly logical elimination of false solutions in order to arrive at true ones—which is, with regard to the eternal philosophical questions, essentially what philosophy tries and almost always, however nobly, fails to do. And of course, education, which, roughly speaking, was Socrates' profession, routinely employs the Socratic method to help students learn in the long run how to answer their own questions. Finally, psychoanalysis and psychotherapy owe a significant portion of their questioning technique to the Socratic method. In fact, Chris Higgins, of Teachers College at Columbia University, has suggested that Socrates' interrogations were ultimately a form of *katharsis*:

> Socrates (who reportedly has no wisdom other than the knowledge of his own ignorance) forces his interlocutors through cross-examination to recognize in a moment of difficulty (or aporia) that they do not know what they thought they knew. Thus, Socrates becomes a mirror through which his interlocutors grasp that they are not in harmony with themselves.

But does Socrates deserve his place at the head of the line of the Western history of conversation which he is routinely awarded? Well, not really. Because from what we believe we know of his spoken words, he nearly always had in mind "exposing" something and/or making a point of some kind—like Columbo. He talked to people for specific moral or intellectual purposes. He could be very annoying, even if in a good way. In fact, it seems to me that he was probably condemned to death partly for first-degree annoyance. The youth of Athens admired Socrates precisely because he got under the togas and skin of their elders—thus, maybe, the charges of "corruption." He was a kind of bohemian Athenian. But after all was said and done, he went around trying to prove something.

So: not much aim-less-ness to be found here. But if, as so many scholars do (and rightly so), we can consider Socrates' often pestiferous interrogations as a form of *curiosity*, and his attentiveness to the answers as close *listening*, then we are at last beginning to talk conversation. In other words, we can deliberately ignore his goals and accord his way of reaching them as conversationally trailblazing. After all, we have no other ancient examples of this kind of deeply engaged intellectual inquiry.

Cicero usually comes next in this story, a Roman bearing not gifts but something like a primary source. Here he is a studious young fellow who would later become a thoughtful and powerful elder.

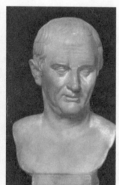

In 44 B.C., late in his life, Cicero wrote his long essay *De Officiis* (On Duties) in the form of a letter to his son, Marcus. As you may know, this essay is widely considered one of the most important documents of our civilization; but if you didn't know that or, like me, hadn't remembered it from Mr. Callahan's third-year Latin class, all you do need to know is that Gutenberg printed it on his press second in line only to the Bible. In Walter Miller's classic Harvard University Press translation, Cicero has this—a primary historical source if ever there was one—to say about our topic:

> Conversation, then, in which the Socratics are the best models, should have these qualities. It should be easy and not in the least dogmatic; it should have the spice of wit. And the one who engages in conversation should not debar others from participating in it,

as if he were entering upon a private monopoly; but, as in other things, so in a general conversation he should think it not unfair for each to have his turn. He should observe, first and foremost, what the subject of conversation is. If it is grave, he should treat it with seriousness; if humorous, with wit. And above all, he should be on the watch that his conversation shall not betray some defect in his character. This is most likely to occur, when people in jest or in earnest take delight in making malicious and slanderous statements about the absent, on purpose to injure their reputations.

The subjects of conversation are usually affairs of the home or politics or the practice of the professions and learning. Accordingly, if the talk begins to drift off to other channels, pains should be taken to bring it back again to the matter in hand—but with due consideration to the company present; for we are not all interested in the same things at all times or in the same degree. We must observe, too, how far the conversation is agreeable and, as it had a reason for its beginning, so there should be a point at which to close it tactfully.

Okay, that's it! Book's done—at least in terms of saying what the most general rules of conversation may be. At least formal conversation, because Cicero's admonition not to reveal one's own defects is pretty guarded and ultimately unfollowable anyway. In any case, neither *The Fine Art of Small Talk* by Debra Fine, nor *How to Talk to Anyone* by Leil Lowndes, nor *The Art of Conversation* by James A. Morris Jr., nor *Good Conversation Is for Everyone* by Renate Zorn, nor *The Art of Mingling* by Jeanne Martinet (and I'm sorry, but can we just linger over that wonderful surname for a second?), nor *How to Make Anyone Fall in Love with You* by the aforementioned Leil Lowndes, nor *Conversationally Speaking* by Alan Garner, nor *How to Be a People Magnet* by L. L. (again), nor *The Art of Civilized Conversation* by Margaret Shepherd, nor *Talk to Me* by Carole Honeychurch, MA, and Angela Watrous can put a patch of any real size on Cicero's advice.

In fact, it's remarkable how much accord there is throughout the historical literature of conversation—including these modern self-help books, which more often than one might expect contain truly useful guidance—about what one should and shouldn't do when talking to others. Or maybe not so remarkable, given anthropologists' views of conversation's origins, its social purposes, and its universality. Standing behind Cicero's advice, and some of the purely social advice of the advice books, the ritual aspects of nonpurposeful conversation are easy to see.

Thanks to the involuntarily tireless efforts of his slave/ stenographer Tiro, more than eight hundred of Cicero's letters survive. One can extrapolate at least some of his character and, possibly, conversational presence from them, even though they are written in formal, and surpassingly beautiful, Latin. In 56. B.C., in a letter to an old friend and neighbor, L. Lucceius, who was also a historian, Cicero wrote:

> I have frequently attempted to say to you in person what I am about to write but was prevented from doing so by a kind of nearly silly bashfulness. Now that I am out of your presence I shall speak out more clearly: a letter can't blush. I am afire with an incredibly ardent wish—one that I think I have no reason to be embarrassed about—that in a history written by you my name should be conspicuous, and often mentioned with admiration.

And to his most favored mail recipient, Atticus, a man very well known exclusively for being Cicero's most favored mail recipient, he writes, in 44 B.C.:

> Finally, a letter-carrier from my son! And, by Hercules, a letter beautifully formed, demonstrating all by itself some progress. Others also give me excellent reports of him. . . . Herodes speaks in the highest terms of him. In short, I am glad even if I am being deceived in this matter, and am not sorry to be credulous.

A letter from his son! Imagine! And wouldn't it be great to be able to say, "By Hercules!" and mean it? In these two fragments and in many others, Cicero shows the sort of directness and "spice of wit" that he advises in his conversational instructions. Surely one would hope to sit next to him at a dinner party, with Socrates down at the other end of the table, hectoring someone else with his insistent iconoclastic scrutiny.

The Dark Ages that followed the Roman Empire appear to have been Quiet Ages as well—at least with regard to documents about conversation. There are very few secondary or even tertiary Western sources of material on the subject. In his excellent book *Conversation: A History of a Declining Art,* Stephen Miller says that "no equivalent existed at the time to classical or modern discussions of ordinary conversation." But at the time of the Renaissance, ideas and opinions about conversation flourished, along with everything else, as Europe rediscovered the Greek and Roman classics and as Gutenberg's printing press made possible widespread dissemination of texts.

The two books that Miller cites most prominently with regard to conversation are Baldassare Castiglione's *The Book of the Courtier* (1528) and Giovanni Della Casa's *Galateo* (1558). Both are, among other things, guides to manners. They were translated into English and became enormously popular everywhere, as gentlemen throughout Europe evidently strove to surmount the crudities of the times that preceded them. Castiglione, for example, offers this counsel to the Courtier (in the wonderful translation by Sir Thomas Hoby in the sixteenth century):

> He shall be no carrier about of trifling news. He shall not speak words that may offend, where his intent was to please. He shall not be stubborn and full of contention, as some busybodies that a man would suppose had no other delight but to vex and stir men like flies, and take upon them to contradict every man spitefully without respect. He shall be no babbler, not given to lightness, no liar, no boaster, nor fond flatterer, but keeping him always within his bounds.

The most provocative account that I've found of the ascent, the role, and the practice of "civil conversation" in European society in the Renaissance comes at, of all places, the beginning of *The Duel in Early Modern England: Civility, Politeness, and Honour* by Markku Peltonen. The author argues that courtly conversation was *not* the result of an effort to replace the sudden medieval mayhem of violent conflicts to redress grievances—that is, throwing down the gauntlet at the drop of a hat—as some scholars have argued. Rather, Peltonen believes that it expressed, in its elaborate do's and don'ts (the ceremonial grounding of a gauntlet instead of an impulsive hat), the *same* code of honor and courtesy that governed the culture of dueling. *Together* they were meant to supersede the ungoverned conflicts of the past.

Della Casa and Castiglione were translated into English in the 1500s. (English is the language and culture this history will stick to from now on, in a bald rejection of the stylized Continental salon manners that dominated the mainland— and, more important, in order to finish this chapter someday.) By the mid-1600s, the coffeehouses of London had proliferated and assumed a central place in the talk of the town. From Bryant Lillywhite's *London Coffee Houses*:

The London coffee-houses provided a gathering place where, for a penny admission charge, any man who was reasonably dressed could smoke his long, clay pipe, sip a dish of coffee, read the newsletters of the day, or enter into conversation with other patrons. . . . Runners were sent round to the coffee-house to report major events of the day, such as victory in battle or political upheaval. . . . Most of the establishments functioned as reading rooms, for the cost of newspapers and pamphlets was included in the admission charge. . . . Naturally, this dissemination of news led to the dissemination of ideas, and the coffee-house served as a forum for their discussion. . . .

The patrons of the coffee-houses agreed to conform to the strict rules of the establishments. . . . All men were equal in these establishments, and none need give his place to a "Finer" man. Anyone who swore was made to "forfeit twelve pence," and the man who began a quarrel "shall give each man a dish t'atone the sin." "Maudlin lovers" were forbidden "here in Corners to mourn," for all were expected to "be brisk, and talk, but not too much," and "Sacred Things" must be excluded from conversation.

Dryden, Pope, Addison, Steele, Swift, and many other writers and thinkers gathered at coffeehouses. (Women were banned.) Many such establishments served special clienteles—in fact, Lloyd's of London originated in a coffeehouse run by Edward Lloyd where ship insurance underwriters got together.

The conversationally most famous of coffeehouse patrons was Samuel Johnson, and here he is:

But, as with Socrates, the written record—principally, James Boswell's *Life of Johnson*—doesn't support his eminence in this regard. He too often seems merely to hold forth, pronounce, and judge—brilliantly, but not what you would call interactively. From near the beginning of

Boswell's account, in one of a chain of coffeehouses called the Turk's Head (the Starbucks of its day):

> On Thursday, July 28, we again supped in private at the Turk's Head coffee-house. JOHNSON. "Swift has a higher reputation than he deserves. His excellence is strong sense; for his humour, though very well, is not remarkably good. I doubt whether The Tale of a Tub be his; for he never owned it, and it is much above his usual manner."
>
> "Thomson, I think, had as much of the poet about him as most writers. Every thing appeared to him through the medium of his favourite pursuit. He could not have viewed those two candles burning but with a poetical eye."
>
> "As to the Christian religion, Sir, besides the strong evidence which we have for it, there is a balance in its favour from the number of great men who have been convinced of its truth, after a serious consideration of the question. Grotius was an acute man, a lawyer, a man accustomed to examine evidence, and he was convinced. Grotius was not a recluse, but a man of the world, who certainly had no bias to the side of religion. Sir Isaac Newton set out an infidel, and came to be a very firm believer."

So much for Jonathan Swift, in what sounds very much like contemporary (and ageless) literary jealousy to me. But, though Boswell probably bowdlerized Johnson's relentless obscenities (many biographers think Johnson was Tourettic), and although he was famous for his poor hygiene and dishabille, the quality of his wit is indisputable. For example, speaking of dishabille, after he'd used the toilet one day, when a woman said to him, "Why, Dr. Johnson, your penis is sticking out," Johnson replied, "You flatter yourself, Madame—it is only hanging out."

No, the next worthy English-wielding conversation theorist, for my money, is the Scottish philosopher David Hume—

if for no other reason than that he formally admitted women to what he was the first to call "the conversible world." In fact, owing to what he saw as their superior social skills, he crowned the ladies "sovereigns" of this "empire." In an originally unpublished essay called "Of Essay-Writing," which appears to have as much to do with conversation as with essays, Hume trenchantly explains why the "learned world" benefits from the conversible world and vice versa:

> The separation of the learned from the conversible world seems to have been the great defect of the last age, and must have had a very bad influence both on books and company: for what possibility is there of finding topics of conversation fit for the entertainment of rational creatures, without having recourse sometimes to history, poetry, politics, and the more obvious principles, at least, of philosophy? Must our whole discourse be a continued series of gossiping stories and idle remarks? Must the mind never rise higher, but be perpetually
>
> > *Stun'd and worn out with endless chat*
> > *Of Will did this, and Nan said that?*

In another essay, "Of Refinement of the Arts," Hume argues that the good aspect of what he calls "luxury"—mainly, a sociable leisure—fosters refinements not only in the arts but in conversation. He prescribes conversation as an antidote to hostility and boorishness and claims that, along with other refinements, it can lead and even has led to a harmonious society. He also says that such refinements will not diminish the "martial spirit" of a nation, but I must say he sounds like a Democrat trying to sound like a Republican when he says that. I mean, the conclusion he is heading for when he heads himself off at the militaristic pass is that such refinements can ultimately bring about peace. This is a position, however dewy-eyed and however unoccupied by Hume himself, with which I agree. And it deserves, and will get, more attention later on.

As will another of Hume's precepts, this one openly owned up to by him and in my opinion so central to the general idea of good conversation that I've awarded it italics: "*Nothing carries a man through the world like a true genuine natural impudence.*" It has already shown up once here, and, with its own defining irrepressibility, will turn up again, later.

Who's next, and almost last? We must at least bow across the Channel to Denis Diderot and Michel de Montaigne (the first great modern essayist) as we finally set sail across the Atlantic and then into the conversational present. In "On the Art of Conversation" Montaigne says, "The most fruitful and natural exercise of the mind, in my opinion, is conversation. I find the use of it more captivating than of any other action of life. For that reason, if I were compelled to choose, I think I would sooner consent to lose my sight than my hearing and speech." He later indirectly agrees with Hume when he says, "Unison is a quality altogether obnoxious in conversation." I am not sure, but I think that by "unison" he means "complete agreement," although the word may also mean talking at the same time. In either case, he's right.

For his part, Diderot apparently could not only write the writing but also talk the talk, according to a recent piece in *The Economist:* "By one account Diderot's conversation was 'enlivened by absolute sincerity, subtle without obscurity, varied in its forms, dazzling in its flights of imagination, fertile in ideas and in its capacity to inspire ideas in others.'" So if you have Cicero to your right at dinner, you might want Diderot, who *was* to the Left, to your left. He might come up with something equal in humor and pith to his opinion about masculine love: "There is a bit of testicle at the bottom of our most sublime feelings and our purest tenderness."

Since it was one kind of zealot or another who founded this nation, and commerce that built it, it makes sense that we have deep sermonizing and blunt streaks in the way we talk. Yes, there were London-style coffeehouses here in the 1600s and 1700s. Yes, Benjamin Franklin was a garrulous man about Philadelphia and Paris. Yes, later Oliver Wendell Holmes became famous in part for his conversational skill. And yes, people certainly talked to one another to pass the time of day—think of geezers whittling somewhere in South Carolina or women gossiping at a Grange supper in Ohio—but also to do the eternal work of knitting together the primate social fabric. (Randy Travis, the country singer, says he'll love his girl "as long as old men sit and talk about the weather, / As long as old women sit and talk about old men.") This is the history of conversation that by definition laughs at historiography.

So it may also seem a little superfluous to point out that in New England in the eighteenth and nineteenth centuries, whole circles and societies grew up around a kind of conversation, with Emerson and Holmes and the Alcotts holding transcendentalist ideas aloft loftily. Holmes wrote a series of essays for *The Atlantic* about a loquacious fellow named "The Autocrat of the Breakfast-Table" who is the conversational impresario of his boardinghouse. (An academic named Peter Gibian wrote a whole book about Holmes's ideas titled, plainspokenly, *Oliver Wendell Holmes and the Culture of Conversation*.)

But political passions and doctrinaire sternness and toil and business concerns have from the start defined our society in a way that conflicts directly with aim-less social intercourse. As Stephen Miller points out, John Adams resented Benjamin Franklin for joining the Parisian *salonnières* with such alacrity when he was the American ambassador to France. He had become too French. Sound familiar? Franklin was so popular in France that women began to wear replicas of the little fur hat that was keeping the top of his bald head warm when he arrived in Paris. He was nearly seventy years old then, a model member of the AARRP—the American Association of Retired Revolutionary People.

According to a few prominent European visitors in the nineteenth century, American men spent more time spitting than talking, and when they weren't spitting and *were* talking, they were talking about money. "I hardly know any annoyance so deeply repugnant to English feelings, as the incessant, remorseless spitting of Americans," says Fanny Trollope in her *Domestic Manners of the Americans*. The word *Americans* here—and often in Mrs. Trollope's book—sounds a little like "Hottentots." She goes on, "I feel that I owe my readers an apology for the repeated use of this, and several other odious words; but I cannot avoid them, without suffering the fidelity of description to escape me." And she goes on some more: "The want of warmth, of interest, of feeling, upon all subjects which do not immediately touch [Americans'] own concerns, is universal, and has a most paralysing effect upon conversation."

In *American Notes*, Charles Dickens also remarks on the tobacco chewing and consequent spitting of American men and also often deplores the gloom and, especially, the distrust that he thought characterized conversation here. At one point, he imagines that the men must "expectorate in their dreams." And from Tocqueville: "An American cannot converse, but he can discuss, and his talk falls into a dissertation. He speaks to you as if he was addressing a meeting." Such vaporous generalizations no doubt have as much validity as the rampant amateur sociology of our own day, in which we all blithely indulge, and yet . . .

And yet there is something to it—don't you think?

Thoreau deliberately turned his back on society and de-plored conversations about "the news," Hemingway's fic-tion often frowns on garrulity, and huge close-ups of John Wayne to Clint Eastwood to Bruce Willis to, in her way, Jodie Foster—all of them generally Strong and Silent, or at least Tough and Terse—have filled our movie screens for decades. We celebrate every kind of social hero here, of course; there are too many layers and circles of our culture for us to restrict our admiration to just a few idols. We variously love Ronald Reagan and Ron Paul, Paul Gia-matti and Gian Carlo Menotti, Ahmal and Etta James, the two sets of James Brothers, Kate and Rock Hudson, Rocky Balboa and Sharon Stone, Gertrude Stein and Albert Ein-stein, and Eddie and Marv Albert.

But still, especially among the middle classes, however economically torn and tattered they may be these days, Americans have always had a thing for people who talk little and accomplish much. A persistent legacy of Puritan sobriety and pioneer pragmatism—a legacy now abetted and, sadly, revitalized by overwork and technological distractions. At first radio and television often precluded conversation, but now we have newer-fangled gadgets that interfere with deep human-to-human connection more subtly. That is, many of them—cell phones, BlackBerrys, e-mail, the very machine I'm using right now—deal in what Stephen Colbert might call "conversationy" exchanges that are usually abbreviated figuratively and literally, overexclamatory, and often pseudo-intimate.

At the other extreme from the ethos of taciturn anti-conversationalism stands another conversationy substitute, the talk show. These programs are almost always conversation lite or conversation hevvy—chatter, banter, overt or covert self-congratulation, or rant. How often have you heard someone on *Hardball* or Michael Savage or any of the rest of them say, "Let me think about that for a minute"? Or, "I'm not sure why I feel this way"? Seldom, if ever, is my bet. I think Don Imus and Howard Stern and Oprah, in their meditative moments, however rare they are, come closer to thoughtfulness than do most of their fellow media interlocutors. (In France, there is a book-show host named Bernard Pivot who carries on real conversations with his guests. France. Figures.) In any case, wary reticence, business-mindedness, new technologies, and media gabble seem to me to have wounded the *idea* of conversation here pretty seriously, if not grievously. Even though I know that talk remains plentiful in bars and restaurants, in cars and on hikes, at dinner tables and business meetings, in seminars and on safaris, I still worry that fewer and fewer people know the pleasures and benefits of true conversation. And that is my main reason for writing this book, even though ultimately I'm as practical-minded as any "real American" and believe that good conversation, however aim-less it is, almost always strikes a target of usefulness anyway.

So when it works, how does it work?

CHAPTER THREE

SURVEY, DISCOVERY, RISKS, AND ROLES

FULA GREETING RITUAL

As noted ruefully in chapter 1, after the first time I tried to record a sample conversation between two strangers to discuss in this book, one of the participants, another writer, pulled out of the deal. He said that he had talked too much about his writing and, more important, he had told a troubling story about the obstetrician who had delivered his and his wife's first child. This doctor was subsequently convicted of raping three or four of his patients. The now nonparticipant's wife objected to the retailing of this story, is my guess, and she has a black belt in karate, and he is a slender and sensitive fellow. The second time, with two new people, the batteries ran out or something like that. The third time, with one of the same people and a new person, I failed to point out that the Record button on the nifty little digital recording device I had bought had to be pushed twice—a safeguard against inadvertent recording that in my hands turned into a guarantor of non-recording.

The fourth time, the same young woman talked to a young man who was an impossible bloviator. The fifth time, the same and now hoarse and benighted young woman talked to a wonderful guy who worked for PEN and the memory card in the recorder ran out of space in about twenty minutes. So I decided that if the sixth attempt was going to be screwed up, I was going to do the screwing up myself.

What follows are sections of that ninety-minute conversation, at lunch between me and a different young woman—once again, another writer—interspersed with commentary about what seem to me to be its shape and explicit and implicit content. Some of the pauses, repetitions, and waiter exchanges have been edited out. I believe that this encounter, like all such exchanges, at once adheres to and departs from what I see as the standard structure and content of purely social talk between people who are not close friends. And makes its complexity and pleasures manifest.

Hold on for another second, though. Isn't this experiment as flawed as Professor Uncertainty, Werner Heisenberg, says all experiments are in which the observer simply through the act of observing affects the event he is observing? This is the field anthropologist's dilemma. He drops in on some natives, as they used to be called, and his very presence alters their way of life. They pose for his camera or clam up or as a prank invent a religion on the spot or behave in other atypical ways. It seems as though the project should be even more compromised here, since in this case the observer, me, knows what the results of the experiment are supposed to be and thus will almost surely steer the exchange in those directions. As if an anthropologist believed in advance that his natives had a serious kasha addiction and then provided the kasha himself. All I can say is that that kind of interference just didn't happen, and you'll have to take my word for it. And take a look at the excerpts, to see if they seem natural and unguided to you, as they did to me, at the time and in retrospect. My partner and I every now and then did become aware of the recording, but that didn't happen often, and I was able to banish my own amateur theories from my mind almost completely.

Since a conversation so often resembles an intricate dance, I will self-flatteringly call myself Fred here and my new friend, more deservedly, Ginger. The conversation took place over lunch in a small sushi restaurant in Brooklyn. Don't get your hopes up for sparkling. That's for the likes of Gore Vidal and William Buckley, Boswell and Johnson, Thelma and Louise, Mike and the Mad Dog, and Click and Clack.

FRED: How are you?

GINGER: Good, how are you doing? Sorry I'm late.

FRED: Don't be silly. I was watching the world of Brooklyn go by.

GINGER: Did you see anything interesting?

FRED: Well, it's an interesting neighborhood, I'm just so not used to Brooklyn. You look younger than the last time I saw you.

GINGER: Do I?

FRED: Well, it's so long ago.

GINGER: That's *good*.

FRED: (*laughs*)

GINGER: I wonder, because I had a streak of gray hair, did we meet before I started to dye my hair?

FRED: I think we did.

GINGER: Did we?

FRED: I think so.

GINGER: Anyway that might be it, I think we actually met after I started to dye my hair, but . . .

FRED: I honestly don't remember, all I remember is it was really fun.

GINGER: (*laughs*)

FRED: And I can't exactly remember why. I think it's probably because you gave me a compliment. It was probably some very self-aggrandizing reason, but also it was just fun, so I thought I would try this. It's working.

GINGER: Oh, it's working? Has it been recording us already?

FRED: Yes.

GINGER: Oh, good.

FRED: So, yeah, this is like an atom conducting an experiment on itself. I mean, I know that doesn't make any sense. I know sort of what I think, but I'm going to try very hard to keep it out of my mind.

GINGER: Okay, so as not to steer me.

FRED: Yeah, no steering, hands off the wheel, if we crash that's fine, it doesn't matter.

GINGER: Okay, we should call Captain Sully to help us.

FRED: Yes, land in the Hudson. Did you see that he was invited to the inauguration at the last moment?

GINGER: Yeah, and they got great seats.

FRED: Did they?

GINGER: I wonder—well, that's what I read—I wonder
who gets bumped for, you know, the heroes of
Flight 1549?

FRED: Wouldn't it be great if he was like a staunch
Republican, which he might well be?

GINGER: Yeah, right, he could, he seems so, well . . .

FRED: Square. . . . Just go ahead.

GINGER: Yeah.

FRED: But I also liked, being the age that I am, I liked
that he was of a certain age. I thought, Okay,
I'm an older white guy, I'm feeling very obsolete
right now, and I thought, Okay, here's an older
white guy, we're still around. You know, not
everybody is half-Thai, half-Sumatran, half—

GINGER: Kenyan.

FRED: Kenyan and so on. So I was pleased.

GINGER: I was actually surprised to see how old he was,
just because you think, perhaps unfairly, that
someone with such quick reflexes, I was sort of
expecting some young—

FRED: Right, some hotshot jet pilot.

GINGER: Tom Cruise lookalike.

The greeting here is pretty brief, as these two have met
before. But usually, we meet strangers with two conflicting
"programs": the social desire to be liked and an increasingly vestigial, often counterproductive, tribe-generated
wariness of outsiders. After showing each other that we're

not armed and wish to be friendly, with a handshake or a semihug and an air kiss, the best next move is to fall back on pure verbal convention, so that the anxiety we feel doesn't express itself as hostility or too much information too soon.

I mean, so that this kind of thing doesn't happen: A friend of mine, a writer, was to meet and have lunch with a magazine editor who wanted her magazine to publish an article about the writer's first novel. After they shook hands and my friend sat down at the table in the restaurant, the editor said, "Oh, I thought you would look younger." (The exact, and exactly unacceptable, opposite of Fred's compliment to Ginger.) Or this: Once, in publishing, when I was interviewing people to be my assistant, one candidate said, in answer to my first question, about his education, "Well, after my second nervous breakdown, I went back to college and . . ." Maybe that's not a greeting as such, but still, at the very start of our conversation, despite its amusing candor, it was a pause giver at the very least. Or this: A woman I know went on a fence-mending visit to the house of another woman with whom she'd had a rivalry. The acquaintance opened the door and said, "I would shake hands, of course, but my hands are wet—I just finished washing my diaphragm." Or this: When a boyish-looking female writer at *The New Yorker* first met Eleanor Gould, the magazine's famous stylist and something of a myopic sociophobe, at least at work, Eleanor said, "Are you a man?"

We don't need wit or brilliance to say hello. We don't

have to be like the Rhodes Scholarship candidate who tripped and fell as he walked into the room at the University Club in New York to be interviewed by the eminences gathered there. This young man picked himself up, dusted himself off, and said, "Looks as though I've fallen into good company." Despite that counterexample, most mistakes made on first encounters result from trying too hard to impress or to be original or to be "honest." "It's good to meet you" is an excellent start. "How are you?"—as Fred and Ginger say to each other—is okay, but be prepared for a recitation of ills (an organ recital, as I call it) from someone, even a stranger, who decides that your question is not rhetorical. The late Freddie Packard, husband of the late Eleanor "Are you a man?" Gould and a terrific hypochondriac, once replied to "How are you?" with "Not too well, I'm afraid—you see, I have these two colds."

HANDSHAKES

REGULAR HANDSHAKES should be firm, but not too firm. Listen to the hilarious and literarily underrated Emily Post on this subject:

> A handshake often creates a feeling of liking or of irritation between two strangers. Who does not dislike a "boneless" hand extended as though it were a spray of sea-weed, or a miniature boiled pudding? It is equally annoying to have one's hand clutched

aloft in grotesque affectation and shaken violently sideways, as though it were being used to clean a spot out of the atmosphere. What woman does not wince at the viselike grasp that cuts her rings into her flesh and temporarily paralyzes every finger?

Those were the days: flesh, boiled puddings, *grasps*.

Like conventions of all kinds, ordinary greetings, when they are used correctly, don't preclude the extraordinary. They don't hinder good conversations but often help to foster them. They are like the tuxedos at a formal event, which establish that at least at the start we're in agreement about comportment and attire. The variations—interesting ones, we hope—will emerge later. Of course, there are sometimes cultural differences to be observed. In the recent movie *Traitor*, a Muslim American character played by Don Cheadle informs an FBI man that Muslims not only end but *start* a conversation with "*Salaam Alaykum*." But most native speakers will at least for a time easily, and often mirthfully, forgive mistakes in manners made by a newcomer.

The formalities and conventions in first encounters, as in attire, exist not only to establish equal and similar footing, but, paradoxically, to calm the huge waves of new and unique information that flood us about each other right from the beginning. We instantaneously register demeanor, accent, odor, body language, grooming, clothing, gait, teeth, skin color, somatotype, posture, cleanliness, breath, tension, confidence, and so on. Facial appearances and expressions all by themselves usually vary so widely and dramatically that they are like inexhaustibly numerous paint chips. This is why tuxedos may actually serve to *increase* a man's individuality rather than decrease it. So "normal" greetings, like "normal" people, are in fact never normal—if what is meant by that word is non-unique.

To convey our singularities, we don't need to dress flamboyantly, we don't need to say something quotable, we don't need to grab someone's large nose and say, "Hey, I like this." That particular grasp, as Emily Post might call it, actually happened—to me, when I first met a well-known photographer. But he could get away with it, because artists are allowed latitude for of this kind of startling remark.

An arty photographer can grasp a nose, we might endure a comedian's joke about our appearance ("Nice shoes—for an Inuit," a humor writer once said to me shortly after we were introduced), and we can pardon or at least understand an obviously eccentric person's clumsy greeting or famous person's self-absorption or powerful person's distracted inattention; but chances are such forbearances will not earn us a good conversation in return. With notable exceptions, such people may impress or entertain or even dazzle us for a while, but ultimately they won't prove to be good at friendship. They play in a different and often lonely league.

The right kind of compliment is always welcome. After all, "My compliments" means what it says, even though it long ago became a mere formality. "I've heard so much about you" is fine. As long as a) we have, and b) it was good. "I've been looking forward to meeting you" is fine. As long as a) we have, and b) we know for an etched-in-stone fact that we haven't met the person previously. "You look great" is fine. As long as a) the person looks at least okay, b) we know the person fairly well, or c) we know the person has been ill and seems recovered.

A little but not much riskier are more specific remarks about appearance. "What a wonderful tie!" is fine. As long as a) the other person is wearing a tie, and b) it is by our standards indeed wonderful. "Nice shirt," "Handsome briefcase," "What an interesting bracelet," and so on—all similarly fine, with similar hedges. In fact, such compliments often lead to a quick beginning of real conversations, as they may involve stories about acquisition ("I got it from a stall on Fourteenth Street"), family ("It was my mother's—she bought it from one of those street vendors on Fourteenth Street"), or even romance ("Oh, thanks—I bought it for my sister from a young woman who had one of those stalls on Fourteenth Street, asked her to try it on for me, and fell in love. We just had our first kid").

If we're meeting someone of some noteworthy accomplishment, especially a recent one—a writer, actor, scientist, singer, prize winner, astronaut, and the like—it's not just okay to acknowledge or congratulate or praise him or her for that accomplishment; it's close to necessary. As long as a) we know a little about the achievement, b) our admiration is genuine, and c) we don't go on about it. Why "necessary"? Because people who do remarkable things do them at least partly for recognition. ("That's what it's all about," a well-known writer once said to me after receiving a compliment about his work from someone he didn't know. "What is it all about?" I said. "Love from strangers," he said.) Even if they say they don't welcome such praise, they do. Even if they don't know they do, they do. Even if they seem to brush it off, they enjoy it. Even if they seem annoyed, they're not. Giving praise for a meaningful accomplishment serves two purposes at the beginning of a conversation: putting it on the table, as is only suitable, and getting it off the table.

The body itself should remain off the table and off conversational limits at this early point and probably at every point thereafter, unless a) we're undergoing or conducting a medical examination, or b) we are shopping for clothes, or c) it's clear to both parties, especially with alcohol as a third party, that bodies may matter in other, nonverbal ways fairly soon. Or d) we don't mind discomfort or, in an office, lawsuits and are consciously courting them. Height, weight, figure, features (especially noses, in certain cases)—we are processing all this information internally, but we know that if appearances *do* matter a lot to us in terms of making or not making a connection, we should keep it to ourselves. But we should also realize that judging others by such criteria may well make us the poorer in friendships.

Both Fred and Ginger are clearly concerned about, or at least interested in, the subject of age—she had a gray streak and is now dyeing her hair, and he celebrates US Airways hero-pilot "Sully" Sullenberger's seniority. He puts himself in a class that, especially with the election of Barack Obama, many "experts" say is disappearing, or at least waning in number and influence—older white men. This bespeaks not only sociopolitical anxiety but the fear of being personally trampled on by the march of time.

So this section of dialogue exemplifies not only the Greeting part of a conversation, but the beginning of the Survey. Fred and Ginger are seeing where they "come from"; see Fred's remark about the distinctive unfamiliarity of Brooklyn. And given Fred's early preoccupation with age, Ginger even takes an early Risk when she says that she would have expected the heroic Sully to be a younger man, given the quick thinking and reflexes he must have had. They also tacitly establish and survey their politics. Well, not their politics, exactly, but their similarly somewhat distanced attitude toward the subject. Ginger points out that Sully and his family no doubt displaced someone else from some prime inauguration real estate, and Fred half hopes that the pilot belonged to the Republican Party. Both of these people appear to have a capacity for a slantwise take on events of the day. Part of the Survey. And they are both trying to make each other laugh—humor being the salt and pepper of every really good conversational stew and deserving of its own third of a chapter, chapter 6.

To continue:

FRED: So what have you been up to? You're writing your book. . . .

GINGER: Yes.

FRED: You've written your book.

GINGER: I've written my book.

FRED: Waiting for someone to read it—like me, and others.

GINGER: Waiting for a few agents to get back to me.

FRED: I think you told me that they said, "No thanks."

GINGER: Yes, or they kinda said, "I think you'd be better off with someone who relates more to the dark humor of the book than I did." And I was sort of surprised, because I guess I don't think of it as dark humor, I think of it as—

FRED: Who is Judy Blume's agent?

GINGER: Oh, I don't know, that's a good question.

FRED: Dark, funny, young adult, grown-up, sophisticated stuff.

GINGER: That's a good idea. Yeah.

FRED: Do you know what you want? Should we look?

GINGER: Yeah, we should.

FRED: Actually I have seventy-four menus here—I don't know why, but they're all different.

GINGER: Have you decided what you'd like?

FRED: Yeah, I'm not a sushi guy.

GINGER: Oh?

FRED: I have to confess to you.

GINGER: Okay, so you're getting chicken teriyaki or something.

FRED: Probably—you hit the nail right on the head. That's another thing about sort of, some older white people—they're often not big sushi fans.

GINGER: (*laughs*) Is that a newer thing?

FRED: My friend McGrath calls sushi places bait shops, and he says, "I don't go to bait shops."

GINGER: Oh, I'm going to remember that phrase—it's a good phrase.

FRED: I respect and admire those who like it and know it and don't mind the mercury.

GINGER: I mean, have you ever heard of anyone else actually being *diagnosed* with mercury poisoning? I mean, we're always told to watch out for it. . . .

FRED: No, nobody. Well, you probably know these things, these sushi things, better than I do, right?

GINGER: Perhaps a little bit better.

FRED: Where do you live?

GINGER: I live in Bedford Stuyvesant, so that's almost directly east of here.

FRED: Well, thank you for coming out of your neighborhood.

GINGER: Oh no! Thank you for coming to Brooklyn.

FRED: As I said, I'm getting used to it now, and I must say it is cool over here.

GINGER: One of the things I love so much about Brooklyn is that it has all this culture, it has great restaurants, and so many of my friends live here, but it's just a lot quieter, and you can find quiet and peace.

FRED: Right, also the sky opens up.

GINGER: Yes, I can see the moon!

FRED: Which is a gigantic thing to get out of a subway and see an open sky.

GINGER: Yeah, I called a friend once and I was saying, "Look at the moon tonight, it's so amazing." And he was like, "I can't actually see the moon." And I was like, "Oh, right, that happens in New York."

FRED: So true. Shall we, shall we go ahead?

GINGER: Yes.

FRED: So tell me about your book, a little bit, a fourteen-year-old girl?

GINGER: Gosh, haven't you found this, that it's the most difficult thing in the world to kind of describe a book?

FRED: It is, especially fiction. Never mind.

GINGER: Okay.

FRED: Does she get in trouble?

GINGER: Uh, yes, she gets in a little trouble, she gets knocked down a few times and has to get back up.

FRED: Bullies? Oh, you mean psychologically?

GINGER: Yes, yeah, I guess literally also.

FRED: Does she—is she from New York?

GINGER: She's from New Jersey, but her father works in New York. The book starts with a soccer game that she's sort of winning, and then she kind of screws up and they lose the game, and a few other things fall into place and then she runs off to Manhattan to try and find her father at this diner that he owns. He is not Greek, though—despite owning a diner, he is not Greek.

FRED: Just briefly so that you don't feel self-conscious about talking about your book—because I agree with you, it's especially hard to talk about fiction—is it at all autobiographical?

GINGER: I would say the character's personality and her thought process, her thought processes, are autobiographical. At the same time, she's a bit tougher than I am, and was at that age.

FRED: Are you from New Jersey?

GINGER: Yes

FRED: And did your father work in Manhattan? If I may ask.

GINGER: He did not, and he does not own a diner, and

never has. He is a blue-collar worker; is a diner owner blue-collar? Does that qualify?

FRED: I don't know. These days, politically, he's a "small-business owner" and he needs help.

GINGER: That's right, he's an SBO. By the way, do you like seaweed salad and would you like to try some?

FRED: No thanks—I have a whole thing in the book I'm writing about the difference between men and women in restaurants. It's basically a small humor piece, and it has to do with trying food. Women want to try and men find it very trying, so it's very sexist, but it's sexist against both sexes—it's not just silly women.

GINGER: And I'm down with sexism. I mean, I think there are certain— There are many generalizations that should be made, perhaps many others that need to made and aren't being made.

FRED: Well, I think maybe what's happened is, over the years, same with political correctness in general, you start out in the fifties with a very prosperous postwar American society where there are certain ideals of what men do, what women do, what kids should be like, what sex should be like, what movies should be like, and so on, and then there's a lot of prejudice. Racism in the South is expected—it's not good, but it's not objectionable to many, many people. And then

in the sixties you have this upheaval and then
you have political correctness, and everybody
is absolutely equal and men and women are
equal and children should be—you know, it's
all psychologized, and I think the pendulum
[is]swinging back a little bit, mainly because
of science and neuroscience. Just to take the
differences between men and women, they exist,
I don't think anybody says they don't now, not
even the staunchest feminists, or masculinists. I
think people are beginning to say, "Yes, here are
certain thought patterns, you can see it on MRIs
that women have and they're different. Here, I'll
show you. (*Fred shows Ginger an advance copy of*
The New York Times Magazine, *whose cover story
is about sexual desire in women.*)

GINGER: Oh, we have a visual aid.

FRED: We do, and it was not planned at all.

GINGER: So this is the new one.

FRED: This is day after tomorrow.

GINGER: What is today, Friday? Oh, because you get your
Times delivered.

FRED: No, because my wife *works* there.

GINGER: I think my friend K—— may have written for
her or may be writing for her.

FRED: I do know her. I don't know how, though.

GINGER: Okay. She just wrote a book, or—I'm sorry—
edited a book, which I contributed to.

FRED: Did you tell me this actually, in some e-mail? Maybe some time ago.

GINGER: I may have. I'm always trying to self-promote. I may have sent you. It was excerpted on the *New York Times* Web site. Omigosh, now people are definitely going to know who I am, but that's okay.

FRED: And we have another friend in common, E——. Do you remember her?

GINGER: How do you know that I know her?

FRED: I know because she and I—I acquired her novel for Random House.

GINGER: And then you left.

FRED: And then I left.

GINGER: I remember reading about this, and I was like, "Darn, she gets in right at the last minute."

FRED: But it wasn't quite the last minute. I acquired it well before I had any idea that I was going to leave, although leaving was always in the back of my mind, given my age and the fragility of publishing and the salary I had and so on.

GINGER: Yeah, years, years ago when I first came to New York, we were in a writing group together.

FRED: She's in Portland, Oregon, with a baby.

GINGER: Right, I know. And wasn't it her husband who wrote the screenplay for that, some new movie?

FRED: Yes.

GINGER: Yeah, I was like, Wow, he's doing stuff, because he was in writing group as well.

FRED: But he's not her husband, I think.

GINGER: He's not her husband?

FRED: No, they decided not to get married. I think it's sort of a slightly youthful semipolitical thing.

GINGER: Oh, they're still together but not actually married?

FRED: Yeah, it was sort of a stand they were taking.

GINGER: Right, yes, I have a friend who has—yes, they have taken the same stance.

FRED: My grandmother and grandfather were never married.

GINGER: Really?

FRED: They were Russian Jewish immigrants, very radical, very opposed to marriage as a bourgeois institution. They had seven sons, they stayed together forever, except not at the end—there were some difficulties.

GINGER: At the end they weren't together?

FRED: I think that's right.

GINGER: Wow, they came over to New York?

FRED: My grandfather came here and went to North Dakota to be on some communal farm; he was from Vilna. My grandmother was from a different place, and I think they met finally in New York. And my grandfather finally settled down and started a textile factory in New Jersey, which they ran on socialist principles, profit sharing with the workers. It was all very idealistic and progressive. But anyway, yeah, they were ideologically against marriage.

GINGER: Because it sort of commodifies a woman—what was their—

FRED: I think they thought—I think they were sort of semianarchists and they thought that state, government, did not need to ratify any personal matters, that it was a . . . a sign of bourgeois state oppression of a kind.

GINGER: And of course the friends of mine who are common-law married, but not actually married, they've been together for, you know, fifteen years, and the reason they never got married is because the female in the dyad—both her parents are divorced, so she has this almost superstitious feeling . . .

FRED: In E——'s case, her mother died, so—

GINGER: Right, I remember that. And the book?

FRED: I think it's highly fictionalized, but very close to the emotional bone. It's about a weekend in which a woman with cancer is taken by her family to a resort in New Hampshire, and it's from the point of view of the woman, her husband, and the daughter, and it's quite beautiful.

GINGER: And her mother died when she was in—

FRED: In college.

GINGER: In college, yeah, I remember she was writing about that in the book group, actually, the writing group, whatever.

FRED: Right, and that essay went on to be anthologized, I think. So, how Greek are you?

GINGER: Not at all.

FRED: You're Irish?

GINGER: Yes.

FRED: On both sides?

GINGER: Yes.

FRED: And how recently Irish are you?

GINGER: My father is from Ireland.

FRED: Whereabouts?

GINGER: The county of Galway.

FRED: Oh, nice.

GINGER: Yeah, beautiful.

FRED: Beyond beautiful. . . .

GINGER: Beyond beautiful. It's getting built up because of tourism, but—

FRED: Galway city is almost magical, I think.

GINGER: I do, too.

FRED: [*phone rings*] Excuse me—this never happens. In fact, I think I won't answer it. I left it on only for you. I hate it.

GINGER: That's okay. But my father is from the country, the county, the coast.

FRED: Have you been there a lot?

GINGER: I've been there five or so times, but I haven't been back since I was twenty-five.

FRED: Last year.

GINGER: Right, and I'd like to go back. My grandfather lived there, and he just passed away over the summer. But, yeah, it's too bad all the old relatives are passing away, because they really represent the old world and a really different lifestyle and experience. And my dad is from there, and my mom's parents are both from there.

FRED: From Galway as well?

GINGER: No, from Roscommon and Mayo.

FRED: Well, it's my favorite place in the world. And I also am a great fan, to the chagrin of many people I know, of Irish music, and when I was editing Billy Collins—

GINGER: Cool.

FRED: Yes, to drop a name, who is Irish obviously, in descent, and I was talking about that, and he said, "You mean you *like* that jiggity-jig shit?"

GINGER: And you do!

In this section of the conversation, what I've termed the Survey continues and expands. For rather a long time, I must admit, even in this redacted version. Remember that the actual meeting was ninety minutes long, so I've tried to distill it into a concentrate without altering its basic shape or content. Like the human body, conversations of this open-ended sort do have basic similarities, as I've said, but also like our physiognomies, each one is different, frequently wildly so. Just think of Kate Moss and Shaquille O'Neal.

And as almost always happens, the Survey leads to the Discovery of common ground. A lot of common ground. Some of it is obvious and has been, at least until lately, a distinctly American kind—namely, the recent immigrant histories of Fred's and Ginger's families. They also share a love of Ireland, even if for different reasons. They have a pretty close mutual friend, they are both writers, the friend is a writer, they can chatter on about the business of writing and publishing. And they do, don't they?

A more interesting commonality here emerges from something unsaid rather than said: Neither Fred nor Ginger makes any judgment about unmarried couples, past or present, having children. They mention three different instances of this phenomenon without censure. Or approval, come to think of it. They silently agree that they view this kind of subject as at once sociologically interesting but morally neutral. And that is a telling Discovery which almost certainly represents other wide areas of social-issue agreement, including one that appears openly in the talk, about the differences between men and women. "I'm down with sexism," Ginger says.

In a couple of places, Ginger begins to take a Risk—in mid-Survey. She implicitly admits to a touch of jealousy about their friend's book contract and, later, her boyfriend's movie work. Here and elsewhere—about agents, for example—she gives some evidence of professional insecurity (as will come as no surprise to her). But even though she makes this confession briefly and quietly, it carries even more freight, in the form of trust, than might first be apparent. Fred also takes a mild Risk, with some hemming and hawing, by referring to the potentially contentious subject of gender differences. This, too, provides evidence of trust. He may make his one dropped name, the poet Billy Collins, hit the ground with much more of a thump than it would have if he hadn't tried to post-admit the name-dropping. But the tardy attempt at self-effacement is an unconscious Risk, too, because it contains "I can be very annoying in this way."

A pause here to discuss name-dropping. If you really know some famous people or some prominent people in your community and they're your friends, using their names is not dropping their names. It's the difference between picking flowers from your own garden and ordering from Teleflora. If a point in the conversation you're having requires that you refer to a famous or well-recognized person as a friend, and if the famous person *is* a friend, refer to the famous person as a friend and then move on. Don't worry, as Fred does, self-consciously, about how the name will be received. Expressing that worry will instantly turn a mentioned name into a dropped name. If you're not a name-dropper, the person you're talking to will realize that and will tolerate the random appearance of a cognoscente, glitterato, literato, celeb, politico, and the like when it makes conversational sense.

I know some professionals at this sport who make Fred look like a hopeless duffer. I recently got an e-mail in which the sender, a hobnobber whose suits look seriously worn at the shoulders from so much rubbing, criticized the musicianship of a very famous actor when he gave a brief performance on the piano after dinner—"at our house last night." That little name-dropping grenade exploded at the end of the sentence because the sender meant it to look like the least important part of the message. See, this is the way the pros get away with it, or think they get away with it. They wrap the pig of name-dropping in a blanket of casualness, or even criticalness, and seem to actually believe that you won't taste the inner wiener. But tell me, which does your palate register more strongly, the blanket or the pig?

Another person, an ex-colleague of mine, just goes ahead and litters the ground with famous names as a flower girl at a wedding strews petals at the start of the procession. She drops so many names that you hardly notice it after a while, like rain on the roof. It is a marvel. The best single piece of name-dropping I've ever heard came from an old artist I consider a good friend, even though he often commits this conversational sin. We were talking about plays we'd seen, and I had confessed to not liking live theater much, but, after giving me a long list of plays he'd enjoyed (and just parenthetically, sort of like this, stars he'd met), he pressed me to tell him what I thought was the best play I'd ever attended. I said, "Well, it was a very long time ago, but I'd say it was Richard Burton in *Hamlet* on Broadway." "Oh, yes!" my friend said. "That production started out in London, and he *told* me how much better American audiences were." My friend had achieved the pinnacle of his art—pronoun-dropping.

Overall, Ginger lends modern credence to David Hume's antique position that women are the "sovereigns" of the "conversible world." It's a lovely touch when to Fred's "You probably know these sushi things better," she replies, "Perhaps a little bit better." And instead of saying, near the start, "Oh it's so hard to talk about fiction" or something like that, she instead *asks,* "Gosh, haven't you found that it's the most difficult thing in the world to describe a book?" Fred's two extended speeches—one about his grandparents and the other his intellectually suspect sociological history of sexism in America—do indicate what I've found to be a male tendency to perform something like set-pieces, which, I can tell you with some Frederickian authority, these were. And he interrupts more. I'm beginning to think he needs to mend some of his ways, charming though he obviously is. Let's see if he does, in

CHAPTER FOUR

LIEBE UND ARBEIT
(BUT, TO BE HONEST, REALLY
JUST THE REST OF CHAPTER 3)

To CONTINUE:

GINGER: And you do ["like that jiggity-jig shit" Irish
music—remember?]!

FRED: I do, I like it okay, I like better versions of it, but
I do like it.

GINGER: Do you put it on at home?

FRED: Absolutely, absolutely.

GINGER: Wow. I like the people playing the fiddle in the corner when I'm in a bar, in Ireland.

FRED: Yeah, yeah, but you would never pick it up. What do you listen to? What do you put on?

GINGER: I listen to a lot of indie rock, which I'm sure you don't listen to.

FRED: I listen to a fair share.

GINGER: In fact in my novel there is Arcade. Do you like the Arcade Fire?

FRED: Yes, basically because my children told me about it. I've just written a piece about Neko Case.

GINGER: Oh, cool! What's your piece about?

FRED: It's about her. I mean, she has a new CD coming out.

GINGER: So it's just sort of a profile?

FRED: I went out to Tucson, to see her.

GINGER: Gosh, you have the best life! Don't you?

FRED: I have a pretty good life. Well, given the human condition I have a pretty good life.

GINGER: Which I will take as a given. That's pretty great. What did you think of her?

FRED: I like her music. I think she has an amazing voice, as many other people do. This is honestly a big deal for her, to have a feature in the *Times Magazine,* it makes a big difference to somebody like that, not that she wasn't

already successful, 'cause each album has
gotten—

GINGER: Bigger and bigger.

FRED: But I did a very short thing about Jerry Douglas
about five years ago, the Dobro player for Alison
Krauss.

GINGER: Oh, okay.

FRED: The guy who does the slide guitar. And I said,
"I'm not, you know, your *flack*. I'm sort of a
journalist." And he said, "I don't care—you
doubled my fees." That's how important a piece
in the *Times* is. So—I ask this question all the
time, and it's not just for this device here: What
do you do when you wake up in the morning?
Where do you go? Do you write? Do you go to
an office ever?

GINGER: My life's a little off the map right now, and I feel
like it's time to get back on the map, but it's a
weird time to try get back up. We may be moving
into career advice mode right now—is that okay?

FRED: That's okay, sure.

GINGER: Okay, yeah, so I— Usually I wake up and, you
know, go straight to my computer, basically. My
life is completely computer-centric, to, to a fault,
I'm sure.

FRED: Right.

GINGER: I usually check my e-mail, read *The New York*

Times for like thirty minutes, make a cup of tea. I'm on tea now, I used to drink coffee.

FRED: How come? Too hyper?

GINGER: A big issue in my life is insomnia. We can get to that later, but, you know why I think really that I've reverted to tea right now is because I have one of those little sort of espresso makers. That's how I make my coffee every morning. You put the water in the bottom, the coffee in the middle . . .

FRED: My son asked for that for Christmas—I know exactly what it is.

GINGER: And it's so much work to clean it, and I think it's just so much easier to heat up the water and let the kettle whistle.

FRED: You use a kettle? How old-fashioned—you don't put it in the microwave?

GINGER: I don't own a microwave. My father has all these sort of funny superstitions about what kills you, and what you should eat. So now I have all these funny superstitions. I think that kind of grows out of the Catholic experience. He was raised very strictly Catholic, growing up in Ireland.

FRED: Is he still?

GINGER: Well, he goes to church every Sunday.

FRED: That's pretty strict. Do you?

GINGER: Oh no, no.

FRED: Do you have brothers or sisters?

GINGER: I have one sister. Do you try to— Are you one of those people who tries to guess whether a person is—where they stand in the whole sibling ladder?

FRED: No, I'm just one of those people who's nosy and tries to find out everything he can.

GINGER: I am, too. I am, too, although it's always funny talking to another journalist, because I usually revert to the one that is asking questions. But when you're with another experienced question asker, you often fall into the role of question answerer.

FRED: Right, or we could just fight it out, like, you know, "Ask me a question, goddammit" or "Don't ask me any more questions—*I'll* ask the questions." I mean, you're right, it's complicated, especially with the extra layer of reporting added on to it.

GINGER: Which I'm slightly aware of. I felt the need to sort of explain for posterity who Captain Sully is.

FRED: Right. It's hovering there, but it's not. . . . We might have very much the same conversation without this thing on. . . . Are you close to your sister?

GINGER: Um . . .

FRED: Edit it out—no.

GINGER: Okay: I love my sister, but she's a very—she's far . . . I mean, she's a far—I think probably kinder,

better-hearted person, than I am, probably, but
we don't have that much in common.

FRED: It's hardly scandalous.

GINGER: What's that?

FRED: That's hardly scandalous.

GINGER: Right, I feel, I do feel—the word *alienated* gets
thrown around all the time, right?

FRED: Well, that goes hand in hand with, with—

GINGER: Being a writer?

FRED: Yes, but also with what you just said about being
overly computer-centric, and wanting perhaps
to think about being more back in the world.
So getting back into a different world, what you
said about career advice mode: What are your
interests, what are your concerns, what do you
want to do, how are you earning your living,
or how do you want to earn a living? It must be
very hard right now.

GINGER: Because it's so bad for freelancers.

FRED: Because the economy is so hard, and yeah,
freelance work is very difficult.

GINGER: So I used to work at *Glamour*, and then I left
Glamour to do grad school and write this novel.
We first met right around the time that I was
about to leave. I had dyed my hair by then.

FRED: That's right, you were going to the South?
Somewhere in the South? Where?

GINGER: I went to Hollins for a year, and then I went to George Mason for two years. I had this idealized—they both paid me, which is part of the reason why I went to those places, but I had this idealized version of what it would be like in southern Virginia, and, you know, I'd meet a cowboy and bang out my novel in two years, and come back to New York to rave reviews and fame and fortune. But it was really hard, and I was really lonely, so I left Hollins. I mean, I did date this one guy, but—

FRED: But he wasn't a cowboy.

GINGER: No, but a jazz musician who is in the Middle of Nowhere, Virginia. And yeah, so then I went to George Mason, where I studied with Alan Cheuse.

FRED: He's nice, right?

GINGER: *Nice!?!* That's not the first word I would think of to describe him. I mean he's a total sweetheart, but you only realize that about a year after he's been breaking your spirit completely. But I do love Alan.

FRED: He's a Stockholmer.

GINGER: What's that?

FRED: He's a Stockholmer, he sort of—

GINGER: Like Stockholm syndrome?

FRED: Yes, yes, you have to kind of get indoctrinated as to his ways.

GINGER: Yes, and the first day—you know, the first day of classes there, he was doing his sort of gruff breaking everyone down, telling one guy Nabokov wasn't worth reading.

FRED: Oh my gosh, I just don't believe that he said that.

GINGER: I'm probably misquoting him a bit, but he did strike down Nabokov in some way.

FRED: He's being iconoclastic about idols, probably.

GINGER: And I thought, I've been through Catholic school—I don't need this! Like, I've done this already, forget it!

FRED: Where'd you go to school?

GINGER: We grew up near each other—I grew up in Bergen County in New Jersey, and you grew up in Rockland County.

FRED: I went to high school in Rockland County. I grew up— First of all, I haven't grown up, which is very important. But yeah, I went to grade school and some junior high in New York, in the Village; and then we moved to Nyack and I went to the rest of junior high and high school there, so it's split. But yeah, I know Bergen County, you're quite right. And when I was eighteen, the drinking age in New York was eighteen, and—we talked about this—the drinking age in New Jersey was twenty-one, and everyone from Bergen County would come to Rockland County and get drunk.

GINGER: I think we were still doing that in high school.

FRED: And get in fights.

GINGER: Rabble.

FRED: Just be bad New Jersey people, that we would have to kill, basically. What town?

GINGER: Closter.

FRED: Oh yeah, Closter. My parents used to commute on the Red and Tan bus lines, and Closter is on that line—that's where I know it from. So, and you went to Catholic school there?

GINGER: Yes, well, in Demarest, the next town over.

FRED: And where did you go to college?

GINGER: I went to Dartmouth, also a fairly conservative place.

FRED: Right, and also part of my youth, because my late brother went to Dartmouth and was in the fraternity that *Animal House* is based on, AD.

GINGER: Oh right—yeah.

FRED: In fact, I knew some of those people in the movie. There was someone really named Flounder, there was a room in my parents' house in Nyack called Flounder's room, because he would come and stay there. He was from Oklahoma, and he couldn't go home for Thanksgiving, and he would come and stay with us. These were real people—Otter, I knew Otter, I knew Flounder. There was no Bluto, there was no John Belushi character. But anyway, it was a very different place when you went there.

GINGER: I'm sure—I mean, at least women were there. The fraternity shenanigans have not changed all that much.

FRED: Probably not—it's so cold.

GINGER: Right, what else are you going to do? Drink too much and act ridiculous.

FRED: So what are you looking for?

GINGER: What am I looking for?

FRED: Occupationally, what are you thinking about?

GINGER: I mean, I would like to write profiles of Neko Case, but I don't know how to *get* there, to that point—I mean, for the four years I was doing the grad school thing and working on my novel, I was freelancing, but a lot of it was sort of women's magazines stuff, and a lot of it was sort of whatever came my way that would not take me too long.

FRED: And one of the reasons I picked on you for this is because some of it, as I recall, has been confessional.

GINGER: Oh yeah, I do a lot of personal essays which are very confessional, which I love doing.

FRED: Have you done—have you pitched a "Lives" column for the *Times Magazine*?

GINGER: I have not yet pitched a "Lives" column.

FRED: That's one place to start.

GINGER: That's true, that's true. I have an essay coming out this week in the "City" section of the *Times*.

FRED: Would you send it to me?

GINGER: Sure, yeah.

FRED: You have it on e-mail, I assume?

GINGER: Yeah, they just checked it over with me this morning. I'm going to blame that on why I was late.

FRED: That's fine, women have a right to be late, unfortunately. So you do have leads and connections. I mean, you've been here a long time and you know people.

GINGER: I do, I guess I just don't—I'm not thinking about things in the right way, so I've been doing all these sort of women's magazines, but I want to do something longer, more interesting, like a profile of someone. I sort of feel like the way— You know Matt Power? He writes a lot for *Harper's*, or like Philip Gourevitch, when he was beginning—what they did was go off to all these crazy places and sort of establish themselves as people who will do these kinds of daring trips. I'm just not sure on how to establish myself. But I don't want to go to Iraq—like I'm chicken, like I'm scared to fly to Mexico, you know.

FRED: Right, and with some reason. Well, the freelance world is a tough one, but it can be done, people do do it, and it depends on your budgetary requirements. I think the idea is to do something, try to figure out what someone else *hasn't* done, what you're really interested in, what is logistically feasible, at least at the start, maybe New York–o-centric, where you don't have to travel, and pitch, and pitch to the right kinds of places. I mean, with you, a good place to think about for you, for various reasons, is O magazine, and I could just relay a pitch for you.

Fred and Ginger still have their Surveying tripods deployed and are Discovering more common ground—Dartmouth College, espresso makers, the question of who's asking the questions around this sushi joint, exciting locales like Bergen County and Nyack, and a metaphorical Stockholm. But they're also taking more Risks, and they're beginning to take on Roles, too, as if defining the kind of connection between them. But let me get off this common ground and clear of the Risks for a moment with an interruption about interruption itself. And a close cousin of interruption, subject switching.

Fred interrupts here two or three times. You don't see these interruptions clearly in the transcript, but you can hear them on the recording. Believe me, they're there. Everyone who has ever written anything about the rules of conversation deplores interruptions, and so do I. For the most part. And their occurrences here are typically annoying. I'm glad the printed page obscures them a little.

But more often than most people would think interruptions are tolerable and work to enliven a conversation. In a public-interview situation, cutting off a long answer with a new or rephrased question can rescue three parties at once: the interviewer, the audience, and the interviewee, who frequently looks relieved to have his own voluble sails trimmed.

It happened to me just last night (as I write this). I was interviewing Art Spiegelman, the author of the graphic-novel masterpiece *Maus*, at an event in Brooklyn. Art is a highly articulate, voluble, complex thinker, and, to his own chagrin (or so it seemed from watching his face as he spoke), he *does* go on. I interrupted three or four times. Nobody minded, everyone seemed grateful, even me to myself. The best television interviewers are masters at this kind of garrulousness curtailment. (The worst, like Bill O'Reilly, do it too ruthlessly, in the service of their own agendas, leaving the person they're interviewing looking like a prop.) In business meetings, too—those enormous vats of lukewarm, thickened tedium and despair—a truly businesslike boss will interrupt and cut through the endless baloney of jargon and repetition for the good of the enterprise.

In everyday exchanges, interruptions can be refreshing. The exuberance of "Wait! Wait! I just have to say this one thing" more often buoys up a conversation than sinks it, so long as the one thing doesn't multiply. Children display this expressive urgency in an often charming way, and I think that many of us retain that kind of talkative enthusiasm into adulthood and can and should give way to it from time to time. It's a sign of engagement—not rudeness—when used sparingly.

Speaking of buoying and sinking, Coleridge's *The Rime of the Ancient Mariner,* one of the best-known poems in our language, has always struck me as partly a treatise on interruption—a crucial reading, bafflingly overlooked by the Academy. A wild-eyed nutter interrupts a man on his way to a wedding and recounts at great length a story of marine catastrophe and salvation, natural and supernatural, that makes *Moby-Dick* seem like a warm bath.

The Wedding-Guest in turn interrupts the Ancient Mariner, or tries to, four or five times:

I fear thee, ancient Mariner!
I fear thy skinny hand!
And thou art long, and lank, and brown,
As is the ribbed sea-sand.

But the Mariner will brook no interruption. He iambically nails the Wedding-Guest's feet to the ground and compels him to listen as he finishes out his story of albatross scarves, ghost ships, living corpses, and the agony of ubiquitous but undrinkable water.

You have to have an extremely compelling story to tell, and the AM's "glittering eye," to get away with this kind of conversational monopoly. Otherwise, four or five minutes functions as a monological limit for most conversations. At that point, interruptions are no longer interruptions but crisis management. The Wedding-Guest in the poem is the bride's next of kin, and he goes on interrupting the AM with protests of "I fear thee, ancient Mariner" and tries to tear himself away. But the AM is like a ghost-story-telling camp counselor in a tent with a flashlight and a scared kid who wants to close his ears but can't. In fact, Coleridge says that the Wedding-Guest listened like a small child.

The Wedding-Guest could have tried subject switching in mid-allegory. Instead of saying, in terror, "Thou art long, and lank, and brown," he might have put it this way: "Some tan you have there, Ancient!" and moved on to a discussion of tanning salons. Ancient Mariners and other monopolizers are the only excuses for abrupt subject switches, unless the conversation has ground to a deadly halt. Fred reverses field two or three times in the previous section of his conversation with Ginger. After telling the brief Jerry Douglas anecdote, he says, suddenly and without a segue, "So, what do you do when you wake up in the morning? Where do you go? Do you write? Do you go to an office ever?" And there is another touch or two of that same kind of midstream horse changing. This damages conversation far more than most interruptions do. You can change the subject painlessly, if you do it with some finesse, but switching channels unexpectedly can generate a blank look and real discomfort, for it is taken, often correctly, as a sign of impatience. It is, in fact, rude.

Near the end of this segment, after letting a decent interlude go by after she first brought up going into "career advice mode," Ginger returns to her professional concerns and Fred begins to take on the Role of adviser and even makes an offer to help. But as the next section will show, even though the conversation tree begins to grow business branches, it retains some of its essential leafy free form.

FRED: Do you know how to be annoying, how to be aggressive?

GINGER: No, I'm not very good with annoying, no. You know, somebody doesn't respond to me after one or two e-mails, and I'm like, you know . . .

FRED: I think you have to get over that.

GINGER: I do.

FRED: I have to say I've learned, even in this later stage, that courteous persistence is much more important than, almost trumps, even, almost more important than talent. Talent helps, but simply not giving up and figuring out like triangulating ways of getting to people . . . In a way this occasion could be that, even though you didn't initiate it, maybe you should have.

GINGER: Yeah, I'm really bad at asking for favors.

FRED: Well, if you want to do that kind of work, you really have to get over it. Just as you know that you do, if you interview somebody, you have to be a little aggressive, you have to be a little like in the face of someone. They don't have to answer if they don't want to.

GINGER: I'm better when someone else has sort of knighted me and I have official credentials. I'm better at assuming a personality that is not quite as deferential as my own.

FRED: It sounds as though you want the people who are going to knight you to come to you a little bit.

GINGER: Or. Yeah, or encourage me.

FRED: Or encourage you, yeah. That's me, too—I mean, everybody does, but I've found that that doesn't necessarily work. I expect people to want to help me, and that is sort of like a parental wish.

GINGER: Right, right.

FRED: We're all children—we're all children at heart in many important ways, and so you have to sort of fight really hard to be the grown-up that you aren't.

GINGER: Right.

FRED: So a lot of the problem with writing today is that half of it—a lot of it now more than ever seems to depend on self-promotion. It's almost part of what you *do* as a writer.

GINGER: Right, yeah, get on TV and pontificate about something ridiculous on VH1.

FRED: Do everything, do everything. It's funny you said I have a good life . . . well I do, but it's not all *that* good. You have to work—I mean, so, yahoo!—I get to talk to Neko Case. First of all, big fucking deal, to tell you the truth. I mean she's a musician, and she's good and all that, but I don't get off on that the way I would have thirty years ago. And secondly, I have to work! You have to go and do it, and you have to call her up and meet, and fly out there, and talk to her, and then you have to write the piece, and then you have to make sure— Yeats has a poetry collection that starts with, "In dreams begin responsibilities"—a fellow Irish person.

GINGER: Right.

FRED: My favorite poet by far.

GINGER: I remember, we talked about Yeats the last time.

FRED: I'm sorry to have such a bad memory.

GINGER: No, no, that's okay. There was a poem you'd read to your son because he had sort of fallen in love for the first time and fallen out.

FRED: "Never give all—"

GINGER: "Never give all the heart." Right, yeah.

FRED: Good memory. I still think of that poem, actually. It's a very important poem.

GINGER: And that's my problem, giving all my heart to, like—you know, some twenty, twenty-two, some adorable guy at my gym.

FRED: You've given him all your heart?

GINGER: Well, no. But he offered to walk me home the other night, and I was like, No, it's probably not appropriate. But then you know the next time I saw him, he was telling me about—he moved here three years ago from Tanzania to help his uncle, because his uncle was sick, and then his uncle died of a stroke, and now he's here all alone, and his family's in Tanzania, and I'm like, I should let him walk me home next time. . . . Awww . . .

FRED: But you wrote somewhere about—

GINGER: Yes, probably—

FRED: About—

GINGER: Not giving all my heart.

FRED: I don't know. I just had this feeling that you'd

written a piece that sort of took me by surprise, where you questioned the very sort of goal that you were after.

GINGER: That I wasn't sure I could have a— I sort of say my longest relationship has not ever been very long. Because my instinct is to give all my heart, my heart gets stomped on very easily, so then in, to protect myself I don't want to give—

FRED: That was a good piece. I do remember it. It seemed to me very honest. How did we start on this?

GINGER: We were talking about Neko Case and the writing.

FRED: Yeah, so then what happens, in dreams begin responsibilities—

GINGER: Sounds like Obama should have co-opted that line.

FRED: So you get what you want, and you find out that it is—like all other enterprises, relationships included—work. And once you do it, in some ways the outside of it is glamorous, but the inside of it may be fun and rewarding, but you find out, for instance, that Neko Case's life is not all, by any means, wonderful.

GINGER: Because she has to work so hard.

FRED: She works hard, she doesn't make a lot of money, and it just sort of falls away. I keep on asking people who talk to me, Could you give me a sinecure, please? That's what I'm really in the market for.

GINGER: Me too.

FRED: So if you could choose a job, a "job job," what would you choose to do?

GINGER: You know, people have been asking me this, including Kate— Hi, Kate. What I'd really like to do is work with smart people who make me think and help me to learn. Of course I'd like it to—what makes sense is that it would involve writing, because that's what I know how to do.

FRED: You don't want to teach writing?

GINGER: You know, I didn't want to in grad school, because they pay you nothing and wear you down. I actually kind of managed to get paid by the schools without coming to do any teaching. But I taught a Gotham class over the summer just for the hell of it, because I can be so in some ways—what's the word?—retreating. I needed to, like we were talking about before, needed to be an adult.

FRED: Be less self-effacing.

GINGER: Yeah, and to assume a position. I've always been really uncomfortable assuming any position of power, and I felt that was something I needed to do without apologizing for. So I taught this Gotham class, and it was just such a great experience. Like, I loved it, I felt like my students loved me, I loved them, and what was really exciting about it for me was, I was learning and thinking about writing in a really kind of lively way. It was much more alive to me and invigorating than it had even been in grad school. And so for all those reasons I'm kind of like, maybe I would like to teach writing . . . but I still have a book first, of course.

FRED: That's right, you need to sell your book.

GINGER: Yeah.

FRED: I'm sorry—did you say it is out with other agents?

GINGER: Doug Stewart at Sterling Lord.

FRED: Good—*perfect*.

GINGER: Really?

FRED: Yeah.

GINGER: I'll tell you, I have a little history with Doug. Okay, I'll have to go home and e-mail him, and tell him that you love him.

FRED: Now, is he sort of tallish and thin? Does he have black hair?

GINGER: I've never met him. I don't know what he looks like.

FRED: How can you have history with him if you've never met him?

GINGER: Well, so he—he more so than Cheuse sort of ended my literary career.

FRED: Mean?

GINGER: I had written this thing in the *New York Observer,* an essay, about my career as a pet sitter, because I've done pet sitting all over New York, and Doug read the piece. I was actually pet sitting for Melissa Bank when I wrote the piece, so I was sort of writing it from her place, and Melissa has this really sweet dog named Maybelline.

FRED: Named?

GINGER: Maybelline, and Doug read the piece and somehow contacted me and said, I bet you have a novel—why don't you send it to me? And I was like, Oh! I do have a novel, I just finished it, six hundred pages long, I haven't even reread it, let alone revised it. And he was like, That's okay, just send it to me, I like to get my hands dirty. And I was like, Whoopee! And I kind of felt like he'd gotten me drunk on the first date, and gotten me to take off all my clothes. I just sent it along.

FRED: Wait, right, you just let everything go.

GINGER: And I was just like, It's so wonderful, it needs some work, but it's so wonderful. He's just gonna see what a diamond in the rough it is, and tell me it's a great American novel. And in fact he did not, and he wrote back, he wrote back, it's funny because in my memory—what he wrote back was sort of a dismissive note. You know, saying he wasn't going to take it on, and I was just, crushed. I thought I was just going to throw the book away, but it turned out a year later, I opened it back up. I mean, what Doug said, and what I remembered was, "The writing is excellent, but it takes too long for things to happen," and as a result, when I put it down I wasn't all that excited to pick it back up again, and I was like, just a knife through my heart, so I thought I would never work on it again.

FRED: I see, so that's how— But now you're back in touch with him?

GINGER: Yeah, and I will say a year later I opened up the manuscript, looked at it, and in about two weeks' time I cut three hundred and fifty pages off of it right away, and I decided to start over with more or less the same character. And I looked back at Doug's note a week ago.

FRED: Did you read the first sentence more carefully?

GINGER: I looked over the whole thing.

FRED: Did you read the first clause?

GINGER: The first clause?

FRED: "The writing is excellent"?

GINGER: Oh yeah . . .

FRED: Did you ever notice that?

GINGER: I had noticed that. But he was so, he had written such a careful note, that . . . and it was kind of long. And you know, he was like, Actually, if you want a second opinion, here are two colleagues of mine that you could go to.

FRED: The knife was still in your heart, even though he was trying to soften it a little bit.

GINGER: Maybe.

FRED: Dull the knife a little bit.

GINGER: Yeah, but so I just e-mailed him again and said, I have a new—

FRED: Anyone else?

GINGER: And then this woman at Firebrand.

FRED: Sounds like one of those sort of fly-by-night, cheap mortgage places or something. No, I'm sure it's a very reputable agency, the Firebrand. I don't know—it sounds like some sort of airline that's going to go out of business.

GINGER: And I got introduced to her through a guy I went on an Internet date with, so there's all sorts of questionable—

FRED: Right, I'll think a little harder about other— I really would have to read some of it. Do you have it on e-mail?

GINGER: Yes.

FRED: Could you send me either the first or most important fifty pages?

GINGER: Sure.

FRED: Why don't we just start with that, that won't

take me too long. I do have to finish this book of
mine.

GINGER: All right!

FRED: I'd like to help, that would be fun. I think
you're a good writer, and I don't know what
your fiction is like. I do know that when you
write personally, you have good narrative skills.
I mean, despite what Doug Stewart said, when
you tell the stories that are involved in the more
personal stories you've written, they move.

Liebe und Arbeit, Freud prescribes for a good life: love
and work—both of them uncontrolled substances. Here,
the Roles of informal career counselor (Fred) and client
(Ginger) take on more specificity, and they (so to speak)
speak for themselves. So does the Risk Ginger takes by
admitting her romantic vulnerabilities. She sympathizes
with a young Tanzanian gym guy and is tempted to take
him home. But what lurks here, less saliently, and in its
way powerfully, is a confrontation by both parties with the
inevitable disappointments and personal shortcomings that
ordinary life always carries with it.

The heart of this part of the encounter, and maybe the
entire encounter, is the two quotations from the poet William Butler Yeats. One, "In dreams begin responsibilities,"
is the epigraph to a volume of his poetry. The other, "Never
give all the heart," is the title and first line of an early poem,

and its words fit nicely as the heart, or at least the right ventricle, of the conversation segment. Fred quotes both lines, maybe as the elder at the table or just being Fred. They are precisely about love and work. Ginger tells Fred that he mentioned "Never give all the heart" the first time they met, years ago. What's going on here, Fred? An old flame—maybe Tawnee—but, you see, maybe, as a married man, he feels he shouldn't really go way back in his life and talk about that, if that's what it is. Especially since the sonnet's last two lines are "He that made this knows all the cost, / For he gave all his heart and lost." But he does quote the line. And he quoted it years earlier. Ginger can and does discuss her penchant for total cardiac donation. She is not married and is obviously still unsure about the whole subject.

You could say that the shoe of "Never give all the heart" loosely fits the foot of work as well as love, but the line about dreams and responsibilities fits the hand of work like a glove. Ginger has said that Fred has a good life, largely on the basis of the writing he has been doing. But Fred, like a father warning his daughter away from the actor's life, is at pains to point out what he sees as the realities that jump out and get you, once you part the curtains of appearances. We'll see that these two come back to and then veer away from serious matters in the last section, but right now it looks as though these are the deepest connections and the greatest Risks they've taken so far. I've broken the transcript here because the next line is one of Ginger's most perceptive insights about Fred, and I wanted to give it a little showcase.

GINGER: Well, I've done a bad job of asking about you, because you've charmed me so much, and that's what happens—I fall into the role of asking questions.

FRED: Well, as you say, it's probably partly a matter of your personality, and where you come from and who you are, and it's also partly a matter of being a journalist. And I find the same thing, I have the same kind of conversations, and I go—sometimes I go, I asked that guy forty questions and he didn't ask me a single thing about myself. But I really didn't give him the chance.

GINGER: Right—they want you to ask.

FRED: So ask me a question. You did ask me a very important question.

GINGER: Which was?

FRED: You said, You have a pretty good life, don't you? That's a good question.

GINGER: Well, how's your son? Because I know him, like the tiniest bit, too, you remember? We went to lunch after you and I had our drink, he and I, when he was working at *The New Yorker*.

FRED: I don't.

GINGER: But anyway, how is he?

FRED: He's getting a master's in liberal studies at
CUNY, and he's blogging. Political blog.

GINGER: Really?

FRED: He is writing a very good blog, which I think
he could do even better with, called "Dear
Leader"—you know Kim il, the Korean guy.

GINGER: Oh, Kim Jong-il.

FRED: Yeah, they call him Dear Leader. The name of
his blog is "Dear Leader Blog" or something
like that. He's fine, he's a wonderful kid, he's got
a great sense of humor, he and I share a great
passion for movies, as many other people do, but
obsessive in our case. We get along well. I don't
hear from him as much as I want to, which is
probably a good thing.

GINGER: Yeah.

FRED: Lives in Washington Heights, with two
roommates, and he's getting through his life, at
the moment with our support. Our daughter—

GINGER: She was thinking of going to Asheville, right?

FRED: Yes, and we went down there so I could listen to
music—that was the main reason.

GINGER: Oh, right. How is Asheville?

FRED: Wonderful, wonderful, beautiful, and all kinds
of great alternative country music. They have
three or four venues, all kinds of Appalachian
music—or, as they say, Appalachan music.

GINGER: Do you like Joanna Newsom?

FRED: Don't know her.

GINGER: Oh.

FRED: I think I do know the name. In fact, I can't remember, I think someone else suggested her to me. I am a dilettante.

GINGER: Aren't we all?

FRED: No, but really, in this music, you read *Spin,* you read *Rolling Stone,* there are people who know everything. And I'm like an amateur, I don't know what I'm talking about, honestly. Unless I write a memoir. That's what I'd like to do next. Anyway, our daughter's a senior at Bates—she didn't go to the University of North Carolina—and she's about to graduate.

GINGER: Is Bates where you went?

FRED: No, I went to Swarthmore.

GINGER: Okay, which is where your son went.

FRED: No, he went to Skidmore.

GINGER: Skidmore, okay.

FRED: They're fine, and I told you about Katherine, she's working in this new job, and it's really a life of very quiet, you know, productivity and work. And huge creative ferment on the inside, of course. Anyway, that's my life. I have no—there are nooks and crannies in it, of course. We have this place I go to in the country all the time, and . . . In some ways, I'm very happy to be out of publishing.

GINGER: You are? And the memoir, I feel the memoir is a handkerchief that you dropped. What aspects do you most want to write about?

FRED: Well, childhood, but also a lot about *The New Yorker,* because it was so hilarious when I was there—I mean, much more hilarious than it is now. I mean, William Shawn was so bizarre. I was at the Tennessee Williams Festival in New Orleans, and I got done doing the talk and I told one little Shawn story at the end, here's this old guy, me telling some little anecdote. And so then I got questions, and someone said, "Can you tell some more William Shawn stories?" and I said, "Turn off the recorder and I will." And I told three or four more stories. That's what I want to write, that's what I want to write, because it was hilarious and—

GINGER: You don't come off as being old. . . . I just reread *Bright Lights, Big City* recently, and even—you get some sense of it.

FRED: You get some sense of it, but not much. McInerny wasn't there long enough. Anyway, thank you, you know—that was nice, about not being old, because I do that much too much, and I know I don't come off that way.

GINGER: Well, it's true.

FRED: So I felt it was a compliment but also an admonishment, and I'll try to take it to heart. I try very hard not to do that, but sometimes it's hard. My wife says I've been doing it since I was thirty-two.

GINGER: Yeah, well, I was saying to someone the other day, "You know, I think I'm just too old for anyone to fall in love with me now." And my friend was like, "You've been saying that to me since you were twenty-two," and I was like, "I have?"

FRED: So it's a quiet life, but very active. I just don't feel like I'm done.

GINGER: You're obviously not done. Right—I mean, you have so many projects going.

FRED: Too many.

GINGER: And what are you going to write about your childhood in your memoirs?

FRED: Well, I already told you about my grandparents. My mother was very WASPy, Presbyterian, Scottish-Irish. Mary Randolph Grace was her name, so her marrying my father was very odd.

GINGER: Because your father was the product of Russian Jewish—

FRED: Unmarried, and they had seven sons, and they named them all after Marxists or utopians—like my father's name is Robert Owen Menaker. Do you know who Robert Owen was?

GINGER: Was he a poet?

FRED: No, you're thinking of Wilfred Owen. No,
Robert Owen was a utopian thinker in
Indiana or somewhere—he founded a utopian
community called New Harmony. My closest
uncle was literally Frederick Engels Menaker,
named after Friedrich Engels. I had another
uncle named Nicholas Chernychevsky Menaker,
who was a socialist writer. I saw *The Coast of
Utopia,* and he was one of the characters in it, and
I thought, Holy shit, that's my uncle.

GINGER: A friend of mine was acting in *The Coast of
Utopia.*

FRED: So it was an odd marriage. They met
in Pennsylvania, my father was living at
Swarthmore, my mother went to Bryn
Mawr . . . was a classics major, they were
both very handsome, pretty, and they made a
nice couple, and they got married, and it was
a strange—I mean, it was a fine marriage—I
mean, it wasn't a great marriage, but it was okay
and it lasted, but I think it was probably a source
of great concern to both sides.

GINGER: Families.

FRED: And we lived in the Village and I went to folk
music concerts, and I went to the Little Red
Schoolhouse on Bleecker Street, and it was all
progressive, and all Woody Guthrie, and Pete

Seeger and stuff like that. My mother helped found the Newspaper Guild at Time Inc., she was a union person. My father, I think, was a member of the Communist Party, and, like, I think he spied on Trotsky in Mexico City. In the Venona papers—do you know what the Venona papers are?

GINGER: No.

FRED: They're transcripts of FBI correspondence, and he, his name turns up, he has a code name. They spied on him, he was very reluctant— He was almost subpoenaed by the House Un-American Activities Committee, but the FBI man who came to talk to him decided that he was a romantic Marxist who didn't really do anything. My uncle's camp in the Berkshires was so weird and bizarre—there was a boys' camp that another uncle owned nearby. Victor Navasky went to it, William Gaines, the guy who published *MAD* magazine. There were all kinds of lefty camps in Vermont and Massachusetts, so I'd like to write about that.

GINGER: I think the best memoirs, not that I read memoirs, are about things that actually happened and real big stories.

FRED: And a lot of them will not have me personally involved. The part about my brother's death will, the part about *The New Yorker* will to some extent, but a lot of it will be storytelling I hope, just interesting colorful stuff.

GINGER: Did your brother die recently or—

FRED: No, he died when I was twenty-six and he was twenty-nine. He had a routine knee operation, and got septicemia in a hospital and just, that was it, about forty years ago. And I wrote this story called "Headlock." I wrote two short stories loosely based on it—it's what caused me to write, probably. I think people often write stuff because they need to shape it . . . and then I wrote this third piece. It's going to be in this anthology called *Brothers*, and that's what made me think I would write a whole memoir.

So that's my life. I listen to country music as well as Irish music.

GINGER: Well, that's unforgivable.

FRED: I love Toby Keith—you probably don't know who he is.

GINGER: I admit that I don't follow country music.

FRED: Well, you shouldn't. If I said the Dixie Chicks, you would know who they were.

GINGER: I know who the Dixie Chicks are, the only bit of country music esoterica I can offer at this moment is— Do you know "Islands in the Stream"? Do you know that song?

FRED: Yeah, don't tell me, don't tell me . . . Rogers . . . and Dolly Parton.

GINGER: And it was recently covered by Feist—

FRED: Who my daughter loves.

GINGER: She's pretty great . . . but anyway, it's a good cover.

FRED: I don't mean to rush off, but I assume you have things to do, and I have things to do.

GINGER: I think that guy's chair maybe is on your scarf.

FRED: It is, but this is a five-dollar scarf from the street, as you may have been able to guess.

GINGER: I would never have guessed. My cousin made this.

FRED: Nice—so do you have a big extended family?

GINGER: No, not at all. . . .

FRED: And have you traveled at all? Recently, have you been anywhere?

GINGER: I have not been anywhere recently.

FRED: Into Manhattan recently?

GINGER: I've been to Manhattan a few times. Yeah, trying to think—it's been a long time since I've been anywhere. How about you?

FRED: Just Tucson. . . . I went to Copenhagen, not this last Christmas, but the one before, 'cause my daughter was an exchange student there and we all went. There was no sun, and it was—it was interesting, it was fine. No, I'm not a great traveler.

GINGER: By the way, speaking of memoirs, I just read James Salter—two James Salter novels. And he wrote that memoir *Burning the Days*. Have you read that?

FRED: No. You know, I know him a little bit . . . and I really admire his writing tremendously, but I'm often left slightly puzzled by it. I don't get his sort of point of view. There's often to me a kind of—

GINGER: Restraint. . . . It's a bit, it's a bit uneven. The parts about him being a fighter pilot are really boring, but it's good.

FRED: Yes—oh, the tedious life of the fighter pilot. I know what you mean. I'm going to turn this off. Thank you—I feel like we should take a bow or something.

The conclusion of this conversation did not come nearly as abruptly as Fred's "I don't mean to rush off" would seem to indicate. For one thing, the conversation continues for a little while—obviously. For another, I've edited out various waitperson communications. Third, you can't see Fred and Ginger making the physical indications of incipient departure. Fourth, we don't accompany them outside, where they say their real, and concise, good-bye.

Still, this very last bit does go on and can fairly fit the description of "dieseling" in chapter 1. That is, like some motors when they have been turned off, they keep going. Travel and music and James Salter's writing are like Hamburger Helper—they're there to make the talk last longer.

The heart of the conversationalists is not fully in these exchanges.

But Fred's hasty, long biographical information, supplied in response to Ginger's courteous picking up the handkerchief of Fred's mention of a memoir, is another matter: It fits in with the Risks taken in the previous part of the talk, even though it is more like a *recitative* than spontaneous pieces of storytelling. He seems to realize the deep water he has gotten himself into when he surfaces to try to switch subjects—to of all things country music. It's as if he knows that he has become too caught up in his family saga and has been going on too long.

There are three minicontinuations and extensions of the honest and sensitive subjects broached in the previous segment. One is Fred's love for and concern about his son. A second is his anxiety about age and the way he thinks he talks about it too much and Ginger's reassurances on the subject. The third is the five-dollar scarf and the cousin's scarf.

The son. Well, of course Fred expresses some concerns, but that he says so, or almost says so, is trusting. The age thing—well, you know he's probably not going to give up talking geezer talk entirely; that's what geezers do, unfortunately, especially when they have been doing it since well before geezerhood. But he'll do his best. The scarves—very sweet! Fred trying, self-consciously, to show some modesty—as with his Billy Collins "not to name-drop" maneuver—Ginger following his lead.

What catches my attention most firmly here is a subtle change in Roles. Before, it was mainly Ginger as supporting actor to Fred's leading man, the Adviser, the Realist. Now, despite—perhaps through—his family history, Fred assumes a psychologically more subordinate role. And Ginger becomes a little more like the shrink to Fred's patient. Maybe Fred's preoccupation with getting older (remember that right at the beginning he referred to himself and Captain Sullenberger as "old white guys") has led him to condense his memoir into this conversation with a much younger person. Maybe he is expressing the hope to the younger person, who has her life still in front of her, that he and his story and his family's story will be remembered. Maybe that's one reason he's writing a book about conversation in the first place, a book at all, and maybe that's one reason he wanted to record and transcribe a talk. I think so. And I ought to know.

And Fred's mention of country music, with (at its best) its elemental themes of loss and regret, may not be so blind an alley here after all, especially as it's followed by Ginger's recalling the pertinently titled "Islands in the Stream." You might look at these two people as "Islands in the Sushi Restaurant." Without making any show of doing so, perhaps without being aware of doing so, Ginger appears to apprehend something of this motive in Fred's story and accommodate herself to it. She is a lovely person.

CHAPTER FIVE

FAQS
(FREQUENTLY ARISING
QUANDARIES)

I t was near the end of a dinner party given by a young friend and his wife. I had been asking the friend about a writer he discovered some years earlier—asking him questions about working with the writer and whether he thought people these days knew what a genius he was. I expressed my admiration for our host's "eye" for literary talent and said (sincerely) that I thought the writer would go on to influence all serious writers, whether they knew his work or not. *A Good Talk,* this selfsame book, had just been signed up, and the deal had made a small impression among the people I know; but neither my host nor I had mentioned it all evening—I out of self-effacement of a falsely modest sort, the host (I suspected later) out of the predator's instinct to lie in wait for his prey to amble unknowingly into range. When the prey refused to enter the clearing, the host, aware that the sun was going down on this hunt, had no choice but to pounce on me in the underbrush.

"Hey, Dan—I hear you signed a book deal."

"Yes, I did—very pleased about it."

"Congratulations! [*as if genuinely uncertain*] What's it about again?"

"Conversation."

"Yeah, that's right, that's what I heard."

"Yes, I'm going to give it a try."

"Jim [a mutual friend] and I were talking about it on the phone this afternoon."

"I'm famous!"

"Ha-ha. Yes, it was really funny, because Jim and I both said exactly the same thing at the same time." [*chuckles— now has the attention of the whole table*]

"Really? [*with growing unease*] What was it?"

"We both said, 'What does Dan know about conversation?'" [*guffaws*]

"What do you mean?"

"Well, Dan, I mean, you *do* like to talk." [*re-guffaws*]

Reader, what would you have said at that point, especially if you had spent the previous half hour listening closely and with genuine interest to your interlocutor's answers to numerous questions—and praising him? How thick is your skin, how fragile is your vanity, how well do you take a joke, how can you be sure it is a joke? I'll tell you later on how I responded.

Like some distressed minicornucopia, this exchange contains a tricky array of conversational problems (some of which the host himself went on a little later to suggest the book had to deal with). Many people on the receiving end of this barb, if their feelings had been hurt, would try the strategy of

CHANGING THE SUBJECT

Whether you want to get off one conversational train and get on another one because you're bored, because the person you're talking to seems bored, because the subject threatens to become too fraught (you can't bear to think about freshman year or talk about bedbugs—to say nothing of both), or because there is something else you want to talk about (say, your book about conversation), there is a range of methods available. At one very awkward end of this range, you can just jump off the train while it's moving: "I don't want to talk about that" or, better, "Let's talk about something else." At the other, preferable end—preferable especially when the person you're talking to isn't a friend and you'd rather not be abrupt—you can bring the locomotive to a slow, graceful, almost undetectable stop. To do this requires having listened actively to the other person and yourself, for its success depends on picking up a thread (left loose, preferably, by the other person) from earlier on in the conversation.

After the exchange just presented, I could have said, for example, "Do you get to see Jim often?" or, "The telephone—how quaint!" or, "What are *you* working on these days?" or, "Was the writer known for his conversation?" Or, "You and Jim should consider a duetting career." Or, farther afield but still picking up an implicit thread, "Speaking of talking, are you talking to someone about your interpersonal difficulties?" In any case, my frenemy's utterly ridiculous, unfair, baseless, meretricious, unfounded, profoundly mistaken, groundless, gratuitous, unjustified, laughable, *risible* characterization of me as a windbag raises another common conversational issue:

BOREDOM

THERE WAS A GUY in college with me who wanted to keep in touch after graduation. He was a pleasant and very smart young man, but he was so boring as to be a kind of genius at it. I'll call him Boris. I swear that when Boris called me, the telephone ring itself was boring. I could *tell* it was Boris calling and would begin to nod off in the middle of saying hello. He was boring because he always, but *always,* saw every side of every topic and wanted to discuss all of those sides. For example: The chorus of a song called "If You Wanna Be Happy," sung by Jimmy Soul in the early sixties (you may know it; it has grown a few pop culture legs), provided Boris with one of his most richly boring disquisitions. Here it is:

> *If you wanna be happy for the rest of your life,*
> *Never make a pretty woman your wife.*
> *So from my personal point of view,*
> *Get an ugly girl to marry you.*

Once, after we'd listened to this song on the radio in a car and another friend and I agreed that it was one of the happiest-sounding songs ever sung, Boris really went to analytical town on it. He pointed out, for example, that the chorus's first sentence offers a kind of universal, axiomatic advice. "Euclidean," he said; he actually said that. But the second seems to admit that the opinion may be only subjective, even though it claims to be a logical conclusion ("So") of the first. Then he pointed out that the chorus vastly oversimplified the choice in appearance of potential brides: either pretty or ugly. He went on to have a little fun with the phrase *pretty ugly* and then pointed out that "never" implies, logically, that one will have a very long series of fiancée choices to make. "It shouldn't be 'Never,'" he said. "Strictly speaking, it should be 'Don't.' *Don't* make a pretty woman your wife.' It may not scan, but it does cover the first marriage and a divorce and a remarriage, because . . ."

With people we know pretty well, tediousness presents two choices: toleration practiced because of the friendship's other rewards—in Boris's case, a profound fundamental decency and unsought retroactive hilarity—or reduction or elimination of contact. With people we've just met, there is always at least the Story of Their Lives. You can prod yourself out of narcosis just by asking them about themselves and requiring of yourself attention to their answers. That's usually good for about fifteen minutes. If the other person can release himself from the bondage of his own boredom long enough to ask for your life story in return, that's about half an hour, and in most cases that should be sufficient.

If you have no choice but to continue talking to Deadly Nightshade—if you're sitting next to him or her at dinner, say—it falls to you to entertain both of you. It's not fair. In adulthood, everything requires work. Marriage, parenthood, parents, staying in shape, listening to music, having a garden, holidays, dinner parties, "fun" of all kinds (except the vices, and often even the vices, especially the consequences of the vices or the preliminaries to the vices), to say nothing of work itself: They all require work. So does talking to bores. So, as with Changing the Subject, you might try to pick up a thread from what the other person has said that interests *you*. If the other person has mentioned New Jersey, you can wonder aloud if New Jersey bears any resemblance to Jersey, or if you're desperate, you can sing "What Did Della Wear?" ("She wore a brand-new jersey," for those readers who didn't know.) If movies, education, or real estate played any part in the other person's life story, you may be able to keep your eyelids raised and your attention at least slightly focused by exploring these almost universal areas of interest. Although the phrases *attention slightly focused* and *exploring these areas of interest* violate the Criminal Prose Tedium Act of 2010, which allows you to take a statutory nap at this point. You can put the book and yourself down. I have to keep working.

Leaving the other threads woven by Boris and his kind where they lie in their coma, here are four other strategies for dealing with bores:

1.   Top Tens. Such lists may be silly and vulgar, and they take a degree of confidence, skill, and playfulness to introduce as topics, but boy, do they work—almost always, even with the least vulgar boring people. Top ten movies. Top ten foods. Top ten novels. Top ten movie-star crushes—she's for him and he's for her, or, obviously, the opposite for gay people. Etc. Just mentioning them as a strategy makes me want to tell you, excitedly, all the answers I would give, but I will content myself with *Citizen Kane,* corn on the cob, *Pride and Prejudice,* and Charlize Theron. Though if I revise this pararaph before publication, the choices might be *The Godfather* or *The Last of the Mohicans,* ribs, *Lucky Jim* or *Catch-22* or *The Great Gatsby,* Jessica Biel or that week's blonde. And it has to be made clear whether "foods" means un-recipe'd straight-ahead stuff, like strawberries, or cheffed creations, like strawberry trifle, whatever that is. One of the charms of top tens is that they often deteriorate into amusing, heated discussions of category definitions.

2. People One Doesn't Speak To. *Everyone* likes this subject, even if names cannot be mentioned. It

will pull almost anyone out of the doldrums. If the other party has no such enmities—and remains incurious about yours—then the other party is clinical and should be sent for reeducation to the Arizona Facility for the Terminally Uninteresting, and you must resort to strategy number four, soon to come. My very informal studies of this matter show that most of us have formed between one and five antagonisms so severe as to preclude even minimal civility. I have two. One is a writer for *The New Yorker,* who is old (which makes me ashamed of myself for harboring this awful grudge, based on a professional insult of the rottenest sort, but there you are). But I *will* tell you that the other person is not the famous best-selling author who once said to me, in reply to my asking him for a blurb for a book I was publishing, "Mr. Menaker, if I even responded to all such requests from you and your ilk, I'd do nothing else." At least he passed the "Mr." test. I tried hard to believe that he had said "you and your elk," under the interesting impression that I had an elk assistant who had joined me in requesting the quote. But I knew it was "ilk." Ilk. Somehow a really withering word. Still, I admire this author and understand his impatience with the literary importunings of me and my ilk and would be glad to talk to him, his ilk, and his elk anytime.

As is obvious, the topic People One Doesn't

Speak To bears closely on the topic of grudges, and grudges bear closely on the topic of conversation. If you are too full of them, they will spring out in the middle of some discussion that has no real bearing on them nor them on it. And others will respond with wariness or dislike. Grudges are like fires in sofas, if you've ever seen one of them. They smolder on the inside and then break out on the outside in unpredictable ways. We also "nurse" our grudges—a trenchant turn of phrase, because in a way, grudges are indeed like infant children: irrational, demanding, "small," and, unfortunately, precious. In "Letter to a Wound," a prose poem, W. H. Auden could be addressing a grudge when he writes:

> The maid has just cleared away tea and I shall not be disturbed until supper. I shall be quite alone in this room free to think of you if I choose, and believe me, my dear, I do choose.

If they grow too numerous and too precious, grudges can turn you into a conversational bore or, at worst, a pariah, because . . . well, it's obvious. Like People One Doesn't Speak To, a few are okay—even commendable, perhaps, because they are honest expressions of strong feeling and admissions of imperfection. And even if you have a few more than your fair share, Fred, and have been told that you do, they are still rich fodder if you decide to write a book about conversation.

One last word on this subject: Lasting social or professional enmities between two people often grow out of the mistaken conviction that others and we ourselves are psychologically consistent— the same person—all the time and that people don't have moments of weakness, misunderstanding, or oversensitivity and that we don't grow and change. We and our ilk do.

And since we do make mistakes, and do grow and change, social wounds often heal with nothing more than time as a balm. It's possible if you've said something that hurt someone's feelings to apologize later and say it was a mistake or that you didn't really mean it. The problem is, some part if not all of you probably did in fact mean it, and the person to whom you said it understood that, and that's why he or she was hurt. "Oh, look—you're getting age spots here," someone I know said to another friend, out of almost nowhere, actually touching the skin on his face that she was referring to. Well, the sayer was not a dermatologist, and there could have been no other excuse for such an observation, not even if the other person was blind and didn't realize this development himself.

This small remark caused some small but real trouble between the two friends, but the passing of time showed the trouble to be minor. It's hard to mend, at the moment, a conversation in which something like this happens, perhaps, but it almost always mends itself later. We have the time to remember that we value other qualities in someone who may hurt our feelings; we have time to confirm more clinically that we *do* have age spots, our children *are* pretty loud, the coffee *was* weak, our man-bracelet *is* kind of effeminate, or whatever; and enough other things happen subsequently to put the affront into perspective. I once wrote a piece about a very famous singer that contained some descriptions and assessments that she gave me to understand afterward she didn't like. I thought the piece was close to idolatrous, but I apologized very quickly anyway. Unfortunately, my apology fell on deaf ears. Years later, we met again after a concert, and this time, after I complimented her performance, I said to her, with some impudence, that if I ever wrote anything about her again, I would submit all the adjectives in it to her for her approval. "Oh, that!" she said. "I was at a pretty oversensitive stage of my career then. You know how it is." "And I was pretty taken with my own opinions," I said, because I had come to realize that some of what I'd written was indeed condescending.

The WASP credo "Never apologize, never explain" does not by any means hold up in anything like every circumstance, but it's a useful vast overgeneralization anyway. A boss of mine whose first job was selling cars told me that if the hood of a new car wasn't exactly flush with the top of the fender, as was often the case with hasty assembly-line products from Detroit, the salesperson would raise the hood, fiddle with the springy knobs on which it rested when closed—this fiddling had no effect whatever—close the hood again, look the customer in the eye, and say, "It'll settle." Well, it *will* settle, conversational contention or damage. This is one reason not to be effusive in apologies at the time of the damage, because the time is too immediate. And it will be a while before both of you understand that you care more about the totality of the friendship than you do a slip of the tongue, however Freudianly freightened.

And I can't tell you who the other person is, but at least he's not old.

3. If neither of these maneuvers works, you might try the diurnal inquiry ploy:

"So what is an average day like for you? You get up in the morning and . . ." It sounds dumb, but it works, Fred's unsuccessful effort in this direction in chapter 3 notwithstanding. Though in one case when I tried this, I got a frank confession of matinal autoeroticism that made the rest of the person's day seem, well, anticlimactic. As a last resort, and in truly desperate cases, when you feel you are approaching rudeness or hypoxia, try:

4. Disturbing Tactics or Derangements. Announce that you've applied for membership in the Minutemen or Scientology, boast that your engagement ring is a profoundly unethical diamond, feign Tourette's syndrome or echolalia or a really frightening facial tic, start talking obsessively about soil-moisture ratios, or close your eyes and ask to be excused because the dark voice of Nee-Kosh-Na-Hoki, your Indian spirit guide on the Other Side, has begun to speak to you silently.

The first three tactics are conversational prostheses or stimulus packages—not the real, organic thing. But unless the person you're talking to is a complete mollusc, they may result in normal social function and perhaps even pleasure.

What if the other person uses one of these techniques on you or, less inventively, he just nods, his eyes wander, and he says, "Mm-hmm," when you've just said, "Oh, my God, there's something alive in your salad!" It means, yes, that you are being boring. If you have *any* suspicion that you are being boring, you almost certainly are, and you almost certainly have been for longer than you realize. Assuming that you're not pathologically dull and simply can't help yourself, the solution is simple, and it always works: Stop nattering on. Five minutes is usually the upper limit for one person's continuous talking. Instead, start asking questions and listen to the answers. Up to a point, because asking questions can easily turn into an interview (which is not really a conversation) or an annoying interrogation, if you reel off questions like an immigration official or a doctor's assistant.

When my dinner host ribbed his little rib, I could have treated it as insult. Whether I did remains to be written. But what in general do you do about remarks that you find hurtful or offensive—

INSULTS

—AND OTHER UTTERANCES that you consider objectionable?

First of all, chances are you won't hear such unpleasant remarks often. We tend to talk to people whom we know and trust and to meet new people who share our values and who for general or specific reasons want a conversation to go well and to be liked. When it doesn't and they're not, the unpleasantness takes two forms:

1. Inadvertent Affronts. Once, in an editorial meeting, an often intemperate publisher I worked

for started talking about the stupidity of all Republicans. I said as lightly as I could, "You know, there may be Republicans in this room right now." (I knew there was at least one.) She said, "Naahh—that's impossible." As with most inadvertent insults, this one resulted from incaution and a failure of imagination. Short of broadly agreed-upon evils like child abuse, Nazis, corruption, genocide, and so forth, in conversation it's wise to withhold opprobrium for any phenomenon or category that may include anyone who is listening, unless one actually doesn't mind or welcomes the prospect of alienating others. Such deliberate provocation makes perfect sense for . . . well, provocateurs—and debaters, politicians, and ranters—but its constant practice will severely limit the range and depth of friendships its practitioner can have. Another example of incautious offense: At lunch, a literary agent asked me who edited my writing at a certain magazine. I had never talked to this person before, but I sort of lost it and gave her an impulsive earful about what I considered the hopeless incompetence of that editor. A chill settled over the table as I complained. I stopped in midsentence and said, "Oh, no—she's probably your best friend or something." She nodded.

Other, less obvious unintentionally insulting and wounding hazards lurk in the course of conversations, especially at the start, especially with new acquaintances, and especially with regard to personal life. The subject of children—having them or not having them, how well they are faring, their possible difficulties, their relationship to their parents, and so on—presents particular dangers. A good friend in his late thirties recently told me how difficult he found the question "Do you have children?" from people he had never met before. I commiserated and said that I thought that in most cases, this was a taboo question. But I didn't ask why in particular he found it difficult. That he did told me enough, unless he decided to tell me more. Information about family matters and finances should generally be donated rather than solicited.

I've called these kinds of tough moments inadvertent, but they nevertheless betray insensitivity on the part of those who cause them. If you're on the receiving end of such hurtful remarks and can remember that they proceed from a fault in the other person's character, even though doing so requires a kind of superserenity approaching genuine Buddhism, it helps. Such moments reveal weaknesses on the part of those who create them far more than they reflect poorly on you. If further exchanges with these people have similarly painful results and few rewards, you should just avoid them. In a work situation, like the GOP editorial-meeting disdain, sadly there is often no choice but to grimace and bear it.

In some ways easier to deal with, I think, is the

2. Deliberate, Frontal-Attack Insult. Once, at a party some twenty years ago, I was talking to a friend about the geographic-origin statistics of U.S. families. I'd read somewhere recently that Latin America had just eclipsed all others, or something like that. Someone else I knew tapped me on the shoulder and said, "It's Germany, Dan." I said, "Well, this piece said—" The someone else interrupted: "As usual, you don't know what you're talking about, and in any case, what I just said is not an arguable statement—it is a statement of indisputable fact." Whoa! This has remained in my memory (obviously) as a real standout, Jack Nicholson–worthy "You can't handle the truth" moment. But its endurance has far more to do with its vividness than with any real grievance on my part. It seemed to me to take place so far out of conversational bounds as not to be a real foul. And most such attacks are like that. There *is* a natural, reflexive instinct to argue or fight back, but counting not even to ten but just three or four will usually show the futility of joining battle at such times. And you can always dine out on and write books about such moments later on.

Not so with fundamentally reprehensible statements. You literally cannot stand still for remarks
that you feel are personally or socially outrageous—
serious, vicious slurs against you or your family or
close friends, racism, revolting and presumptuous
salaciousness. One kind of heel deserves your criticism, the other is made to be turned on. If some
greater essential good is served by suffering these
moments in silence—survival, one's living or well-
being, the polity's best interests, even the success of
a crucial business meeting—they must be borne.
But if at all possible, and for the sake of your own
self-respect, don't conversationally accommodate or
compromise with those who so deeply offend your
principles.

Not all conversational sore points are the result of direct
or indirect insults. They often flare up also when the subjects of religion, politics, race, and sexuality arise and serious differences about these topics exist between or among
the conversants. I'll talk about religion more a little later
on, but for now, I'll say that at the start of a connection
with someone else, it's best for grown-ups to avoid these
troubled waters if possible. Stay on the beach of noncon-
troversy at least for a while, when you can. For younger
people—teenagers, college kids—this advice doesn't hold.
That time of life, when people are beginning to settle on

their personalities, beliefs, and identities, is precisely the right time to throw this kind of conversational caution to the wind. You almost don't have a choice about doing so, since youth entails or should entail open explorations of this kind of territory. And usually when clashes occur, no lasting or significant damage results from them. You "move on," as they say, and make new friends—in another dorm, on another block, in another group—who are of liker or broader minds.

The springtime of adult life is the season not only for bold differences of opinion, but also for the marathon conversations they so often occasion. Courtship produces marathons. "We stayed awake talking for hours," people will say, in one of those newspaper stories about a marriage, of a third or fourth date. And since youth and courtship generally go hand in hand, they double the chances for long talks. As do bars, parties, and cruises. And then, frequently, work and family and all those responsibilities that begin in dreams settle in, and the all-night or all-day or all-weekend conversations recede into the past, as they probably must and even should, since most of the formation of character that they assist so crucially has taken place. Sadly, too, people—at least American people—often feel uncomfortable when a conversation goes on for more than about an hour and a half, because they are so driven to get back to work or some other more practical-seeming occupation.

Back to sore points, and an example of significant damage from a political conversational mistake: I inherited a writer from an editor who had taken a job at another publishing house. I went to see the writer, to reassure her about our imprint's support and my interest in her next project (a sincere interest) and, of course, I didn't want her to leave us and follow her former editor. She lived in Washington, D.C., and my visit coincided with the height of the argument over America's invasion of Iraq. I barely touched on my unhappiness about President Bush's action, but it was enough, I learned later, to alienate the writer—who, as it turned out, was a good personal friend of Laura Bush. Now, it's true that this was not an aim-less conversation, but even if it had been, it would have been a mistake to go out, however gingerly, on this thin ice, this narrow limb. (The writer stayed with us but chose another editor to work with, an editor known to be a genius of opacity.) By the way, Republican literary writers are in my experience as rare as ski bums in the Sahel.

Like family and religion, politics will ooze into a conversation on its own and in its own indirect way, without anyone having to start campaigning or deploring policies or divinities directly. And you will decide, silently, whether the differences between you are too great for friendship and a good talk to overcome. Most of us end up with birds of a feather anyway, especially when we find the plumage of others really objectionable. But it's a true loss, I think, to fly only and always with your own flock. You can miss out on the company of really fine people, and you can fall into a tedious kind of intellectual and spiritual lockstep if you never step out of line. I'm a liberal verging on anarcho-syndicalism myself, if you hadn't guessed, but I find the company of smart conservatives challenging and some-times beneficially mind-bending.

But dilemmas do occur over divisions in belief and politics. Once, a friend suffered a miscarriage pretty far along in her pregnancy and was of course devastated. I did my best to console and sympathize with her, having lived through similar losses closer to home myself. She said she felt her daughter was "with her" anyway, as a sort of real person with a spiritual existence. "Don't you think that's really possible?" she said. I didn't and don't, though I didn't doubt the reality of her psychological and emotional expe-rience, of course. I desperately came up with, "Well, put it this way: I can't say that I don't believe it."

In our country, particularly with the election of Barack Obama, race has finally begun to assume a more inciden-tal rather than central role in our society's conversation, as has sexual orientation. They still divide many among us, I realize—the vote against gay marriage in California a couple of years ago was by no means a negligible event. But those many grow fewer every day, it seems. The tol-erance we've preached for so long we are beginning to practice with more regularity than ever before. And even the unreconstructed among us have a harder time finding safe conversational havens for their group hatreds. I would speculate that they are increasingly ashamed of themselves, and I know that their children share their prejudices far less automatically than used to be the case.

At a writer's conference not long ago, after a reading by a novelist whose books often deal with bigotry and racial identity in America, a young woman in front of me, caramel of color, turned around and asked if I liked the reading. "Very much," I said. "Me too," she said, "but isn't that race stuff getting a little old?" I asked her what she meant. "I guess my friends and I all have such mixed backgrounds that all we do is joke about it. My mother is from Suriname and my father is Finnish, and *their* parents are all mixed up racially, too. My friends and I all think it's much more of a given than an issue. Sort of more of a joke than an issue." An odd upshot of the beginning of the finally true melting of the melting pot is that even stereotypes can (within reason and with caution) be employed sometimes in civil conversation now, because they are less charged than they used to be. Gay people and straight people chuckle openly about gay people and straight people. I remember someone in my office telling a gay man, when he was saying that he didn't think Julia Roberts was very attractive, "You're gay, so you have to shut up." They both laughed. Black people and white people talk about characteristic traits in black people and white people. The religious and irreligious can have some fun with their very fundamental differences. Stealing a bit of humor from Simon Rich, the author of two collections of funny pieces and a writer for *Saturday Night Live*, I facetiously wondered to a writer I know who believes in heaven and hell what would happen if a murderer whose soul was saved ran into his victim in paradise. She was a) stymied, and b) unoffended.

I know it seems odd, sacrilegious, and bathetic to bring up movies in the same breath with religion and politics and race and sexual orientation, but some people feel so passionate about films that conflicts in opinion about them can break a friendship. I think it's because movies have such a visceral impact on their audience that we can feel personally insulted if someone disagrees with us about their merit. They live at the very core of modern people's being. Pauline Kael, the famous movie critic with whom I worked for a few years at *The New Yorker*, once told me that if she and someone she knew disagreed about the quality of an important movie more than three times in any given year, she could not be that person's friend. Extreme, but not completely nuts, maybe. Disagreements about movies, more than books and plays and television, can have a surprisingly negative impact on relationships. Many couples take such differences very much to heart.

By the way, I have read somewhere that the subject that couples argue about most is . . . no, not money; no, not in-laws; no, not child raising; no, not plans; but: *temperature.*

Open vs. closed windows; AC vs. no AC; blanket vs. quilt; thermostat at sixty-eight vs. thermostat at seventy; fan on vs. fan off. That old electric blanket with two separate controls? Genius! Though how would it go if its inventor had his soul saved, went to heaven, and met one of the people his invention had electrocuted?

———

BEFORE LEAVING INSULTS BEHIND, which is generally where they should be left, three addenda:

    1. If *you* realize that you've inadvertently or incautiously insulted someone else, as I did at lunch with the agent whose best friend I disparaged, there's nothing to be done but apologize. Once. *Maybe* a second time, later on—if there's a natural opportunity for re-repentance—or at the end of the conversation. But overdoing an apology inflates the mistake, and it also implicitly makes you the center of the exchange. This is what so often goes wrong with public apologies: They seem self-absorbed rather than genuinely regretful. Harry Shearer's *Le Show,* which is heard on many NPR stations, features an "Apologies of the Week" segment that usually underlines the rationalizing solopsism of many acts of contrition. Every now and then, though, Shearer comes across one that is dignified, terse, and to the point—and therefore much more believable. Such brief expressions of remorse also tacitly acknowledge that what happens next rests where it should: with the conversational accident's victim.

2. By all means, be insulted by insults. Get angry, look indignant, bridle away. But listen to them, too. Even though their behavior may be rude, people who cross the conversational line this way often convey some truth about you that you'd rather not deal with. Sometimes they're the *only* people who will tell you things you don't want to hear but should. To go back to the dinner party exchange, well, guess what? I *do* like to talk, in case you hadn't noticed, and the host's cracking that conversational egg on my head was a reminder to watch it. Again: When I was new as a fact checker at *The New Yorker,* a famously unpleasant writer, angry about mistakes that he had made, got angrier when I argued heatedly with his refusal to make a certain change. "You're so damn difficult to deal with!" he finally said—projecting away like a veritable Cineplex, yes, but also, I realized after a while, helping me understand that I often became too psychologically invested in being "right." From that time on, I simply made my suggestions for correcting what I thought were errors and let the chips of accuracy fall where they might. And with regard to the accusation "You don't know what you're talking about," sad to say, that is sometimes the case, especially with regard to books that I like to discuss but haven't read. When someone asks me, "Have you actually read it?" I now say, "Not personally."

Maybe Jesus's injunction in the Sermon on the Mount to turn the other cheek when smote not only counsels nonviolence, but also covertly tells us to *listen* more closely, turn a different ear, to what affronts us.

3. Never feel insulted if someone forgets your name. Doing so results from vanity or insecurity— two sides of the same coin worth less than a ha'penny. But if you have incurable sensitivities in this direction, *say your name as you greet anyone who might possibly have forgotten it.* Say both of your names. The erosion of surname usage in our modern world resembles the erosion of species and strikes me as being similarly sad. When names carry any interesting cargo at all, it's often last names that do the work. What is Arnold in comparison with Schwarzenegger? Which tells you more, Wayne or Gretzky? Caroline or Kennedy? Amy or Winehouse? Mickey or Mouse?

If everyone followed that advice, embarrassment

on this account would evaporate overnight. What's the worst that can happen if you do follow it? The other person laughs and says, "Of course I know your name." Then you both feel good instead of flopping around like anonymous fish on a no-name dock. If you can't remember someone else's name—a name you know you *should* remember—and that person hasn't adopted the "always say your name" maneuver, I have no comparable insta-cure to offer. But if everyone said his or her name as part of a standard greeting to everyone outside his or her immediate circle of friends, the problem would never arise.

Here's the socially worst name nightmare: You're talking to someone who knows your name but remains frighteningly anonymous to you. You're faking familiar congeniality. Another person joins you, and you are the one who is supposed to introduce the newcomer to John Doe. But how can you, when you don't know John Doe's name, except that you know it isn't John Doe? If John Doe doesn't donate his name but cheerfully waits for you to supply it, even after the newcomer has given his name, you are in deep social trouble. They're both looking at you, waiting. Faint.

Another example of picking up a thread from earlier in a conversation (or, in this case, a chapter): Can the dinner party host's call to Jim—can any telephone call—properly be called a conversation? That's a question that falls under the ever widening umbrella of what might be termed

ELECTRONICA

(NOT THE MUSICAL CATEGORY.) The answer is no. It's just a matter of definition, and many exchanges besides in-person encounters can have enormous practical and emotional importance. "I don't love you anymore" and "I still love you" and "It's a deal!" and "Deal's off" and "You're hired" and "I quit" and "The X-ray was negative" and "I have to have major surgery" and "Let's meet at the One-Horse Chez at six for a drink" and "Sorry, I have to cancel; how about tomorrow evening at the Honey Do?" and "Congratulations!" and "Condolences" and "Your Perfect Vacuum Cleaner was shipped today" and "We're sorry, but the item you ordered, the Handeeman Combination Sledgehammer/Lacemaker is out of stock" and "Thanks" and "No thanks" can all arrive via landline, the Internet, a cell phone, text message, semaphore, and so on. But I would like to define and confine the idea of conversation for the purposes of this book as people face-to-face and talking. Because even if Professor Robin Dunbar's theory in *Grooming, Gossip, and the Evolution of Language*—that conversation began as an extension of or substitution for primate physical grooming—is wrong, it remains true that

the immediate physical presence of other human beings
lends great depth and texture to verbal exchanges. E-mail
and telephone communications don't speak body language,
they don't emit pheromones, they can't convey the specific
sounds of silences, they take place noplace, they cannot involve touch, and so on.

Think of it this way: Let's say technology improved to
the point of being able to replicate all the aspects of conversation just listed—that is, gave a perfect electronic illusion
of the physical presence of the person you were talking to
and vice versa. Let's call the device that might do this the
Conversator. The Conversator senses those pheromones
and releases them to the other party from its FeroBank,
creates a perfect physical replica—a Virtualicon—of the
person you're talking to sitting in a chair (an Insit-u) opposite you and vice versa, and even somehow creates a shared
physical context, by means of its PlaceMatRix feature. It
can even simulate touch, with the iTactilink. This experience would surely confuse any brain conditioned to talking to a person who is really there, but I still believe it
wouldn't live up, so to speak, to the primal human, always
more or less intimate transaction of conversation. During
the 2008 election, CNN tried a crude version of this device by importing virtual images of reporters out in the
field into its headquarters. They were literally off-color,
and they glimmered. The effect sucked. Even the reporters
involved thought it was ridiculous.

There is a reason that "conversation" used to mean "sexual intercourse" and "intercourse" can still mean "conversation," though you'd better add air quotes if you use it that way or if you want to *double* the *entendre*. Almost nothing is sexier except sex itself—and too often not even that—than a warm conversation between two people who have the possibility of getting erotic with each other in the flesh. Women especially will say that even on a far from explicit level, conversation can often be a form of foreplay. Oh, my God, speaking of explicit: I remember sitting in a bar with Tawnee a *very* long time ago and hearing her say, after we talked about this and that, "Okay, tell me what you're going to do to me tonight."

Focus!

Out-of-person, as opposed to in-person, communications always lack one or more of the dimensions of real conversation. They can have their own virtues and integrity: Think, analogously, of black-and-white vs. color photography, travel books vs. travel, treadmills vs. tracks and trails, appetizers vs. main courses, and so on. And they have their own rules and customs, as David Shipley and Will Schwalbe point out about e-mail in *Send,* which I have not read personally. These customs often overlap with one another and with those of real conversation: Almost universally, you don't curse until and unless you know it's okay to do so, for example. (If the person you're talking to says "crap" or if you say it and he or she doesn't frown, chances are it's okay to move on to bluer streaks. "Crap" and "hell" and "damn" often go out as obscenity reconaissance.) You don't make sexual remarks about other people's mothers, unless you are playing the Dozens by mutual consent. And all verbal transactions except for the most rudimentary and functional sort involve courtesies and protocols of one kind or another.

Since so much of our "intercourse" does take place electronically these days, and since you could loosen the definition of conversation to include, especially, e-mails, (if you were more e-evolved than I am), maybe it would be useful to pause for a few minutes and consider some of those customs, protocols, and courtesies, with an eye toward avoiding the small embarrassments and the yawning social abysses into which you can hurtle the moment you hit the Send button. And by "you" I really mean "I," since I've made so many abysmal mistakes of my own.

1. The To bar is a salutation all by itself. Because of the instantaneous nature of e-mail, whose appointed rounds neither rain nor sleet, etc. could even hope to stay, I say skip the "Dear So-and-So." Except in formal circumstances—a job application, for example, or a note to someone not used to messages in medias res, or someone you've not met—it seems almost foolish to use a formal greeting. "Hi," as in "Hi, Jack" and "Hi, Jill," appears to have become a middle cyberspace ground between formal greeting and no greeting. This usage annoys me. Maybe that's because in conversations, which e-mail is so often said to resemble, we don't preface any remark with a Dear or a Hi or anything else. In fact, when someone says to me in person, "Dan, I'd like to ask . . ." or "Dan, could you just . . ." I take it as a sign of phony sincerity, a warning of approaching disingenuousness, or a looming criticism. The great preponderance of e-mails I've sent and received have tended toward the highly familiar and friendly or the highly practical. Neither of these kinds of communications fits comfortably with a salutation.

2. The From bar serves a similarly practical function, obviating the need for a complimentary closing, with exceptions as noted above.

3. Reread every single e-mail before sending it. Every one except those that truly can't matter. Accurate typing is a courtesy that even our closest friends deserve, for one thing, though it's hard to manage on those thumb-harps called Black-Berrys and iPhones. For another, rereading gives you a chance to police out tonal violations, which for some reason seem so easy to commit in e-mails. Flat, clear assertions sometimes seem to bristle with hostility when you don't mean them to. E-mails seem to make some kind of weird implicit demand for a compliment, even if only an implicit one. They often feel more like a massage than a message. But they can also turn smarmy very easily.

4. Does it need to be said again? Watch the Reply and Reply to All tabs and make sure you're not CC'ing someone you don't mean to CC—someone who may be deeply hurt by what you've said or someone who could fire or divorce you. I once sent myself from home a very disparaging message to remind me to talk to someone I disliked intensely at work. It was a juvenile stunt, for my eyes only.

Trouble was, I hit Post instead of Send, and when I realized what I'd done, I knew that if I had created a group for posts, I would be fired. But I couldn't remember if I'd created a Post group and didn't know enough to be able to figure out whether I had or not. I went to work with as much professional fear and trembling as I've ever known but discovered when I got there that indeed I'd created no group and had posted the message only to myself. I didn't speak to me for two months.

Another address danger is typing into the To bar or the CC bar part of a name whose e-mail address you want to retrieve and then give to the person you're writing to *and leaving the address there.* Have I done this? Only about ten or fifteen times—luckily, so far, only with minor damage.

5. The damage was minor partly because I learned fairly early on that like a diamond, or more like the coal that diamonds start out as, an e-mail is forever. And forever forwardable and discoverable and litigable and revengeable and so on. A handwritten or typed snail-mail letter requires some effort to store and retrieve and deploy for legally or personally vindictive or evidentiary reasons. You can burn a letter. You cannot burn Gmail—not even Hotmail. I have learned this lesson, but I've too often ignored it, as have most of my friends and family. As all those famous "observers" have observed, because of e-mail our private lives are often led far more potentially in public. It is just so *easy* to dash off a dig or gossip. This spontaneity is where e-mails' similarity to in-person conversation is the greatest—and the most treacherous. When we, the first cohort of e-mailers, stand before St. Peter, we should not be surprised to have our indestructible e-mail archives held against us and to be ourselves archived forever Elsewhere.

6. Jokes. "Witty" exchanges on e-mail can quickly grow noisome. Try to avoid prolonging them.

7. Alphonsing and Gastoning. Sometimes it's a mercy to both parties simply to stop replying to everything. I've noticed in the last couple of years that polite nonreplies, my own and others', have increased in number, out of time pressure necessity, no doubt, but also maybe out of the general tendency to use a new device a lot at first and then reduce its place in our lives later on.

8. E-Normanmailers. E-mails and other electronic communications between friends don't accommodate what someone I know calls "real writin'" very well, because if in regular correspondence you write something good or powerful or lasting in merit to someone else—a set-piece of some kind—that person often doesn't know what to do with it. It's difficult to respond to, and it seems to be out of place. Save it for your blog. Better yet, a journal.

But, excluding to some extent telephone talk, electronica—IMs, text messages, and attachments—don't demand the kinds of immediate responses that in-person conversation *com*mands, even if those responses consist solely of silent thoughtfulness, wrinkled noses, index-finger ear circling, or shrugs. Electronic and handwritten communications share one radical element: the time-delay capability. It's not only an element, it's a tool. Think of the hero of *Atonement* writing and rewriting his love letter. Think of the editor of a magazine who had the luxury of time to come up with the following opener in rejecting some poems by the late Harold Brodkey, a man he despised: "I like your poems so little that . . ." (A review of Brodkey's novel later delivered one of the most vicious closing sentences I've ever read: "Death would have been a better career move." He died shortly after that.) Think of how many (or how few) times you've executed the "wait a day or two" gambit to keep correspondents on edge about e-mail replies about love or work. You've never done that? You're a better person than I am. Consider the frigid cyber-shoulder one can turn by not answering e-mails whose senders believe they have every reason to expect an answer, and the conversationlike spontaneity and comfort implied by immediate and uncrafted answers—yours or those of yourfriend@e-pistles.com. Think about how finely and deliberately one can choose from an arsenal not only of timing devices, but of tones—direct, oblique, clever, cross, flattering, obsequious, energetic, reflective, and so on. These inflections come naturally, unpremeditatedly, and sometimes damagingly in conversation, but they're often closely considered in e-mail. One of my colleagues, maybe out of busyness or concern about corporate legal policies—or the limited range of written expression—restricted his e-mail correspondence to "See me," "Why?" "Good idea," "Yes," "Agree," "How much?" "Too much," "Leaving at 5:30," "Monday," "Your call," "I don't understand," "Disagree—see me," "Lunch?" "Interesting," "In the lobby," "Thanks," and "See me." "Fab" was his favorite. E-mails usually do run short, because the instantaneity of their transmission and their often overwhelming number put on the pressure for brevity. (More than one person has asked me to shorten my e-mails, as you might guess from the length of this and other paragraphs.) But they also allow for more artifice. Flirting by e-mail comes much more easily—for many men, anyway—than initiating a real-life dateworthy conversation. Of all text electronica, IMs may in some ways come closest to conversation, as they are usually defined by spontaneity. But they also consist of abbreviations and fragments, many of them drawn from a bin of prepackaged, standard IM parts. They resemble the dinner party host's jab, "Well, Dan, you do like to talk," if indeed it was an example of one, insofar as they are, in a way,

PREPARED REMARKS

The french call the remorse and self-criticism about what we wish we'd said during a conversation *l'esprit d'escalier*—the spirit of the staircase. And what about before the conversation? Many of us fantasize about what we would like to say to Barack Obama, someone we still carry a torch for, J. K. Rowling, Henry Kissinger, our awful boss, Mariano Rivera, the train conductor who closes the doors in our face, Emmylou Harris, Ian McEwan, our mysterious neighbor, Stephen Hawking—a question we've always wanted answered, a piece of our minds, or a piece of our hearts. In order: "Are you sure this whole president thing isn't just a glorified writer's block?"; "Tawnee, my dreams are like a small town—I keep running into you there"; "Can you lend me some money?"; "What was that about not bombing Cambodia?"; "You will forever cease saying 'push the envelope' and 'take it to a new level' and 'long story short'"; "Yes, point to heaven if you like, but it's *your* arm"; "&^%#%★"; "I love the way you sing"; "Do you use index cards for structuring your novels?"; "Why is the smoke from your chimney green?"; and "Why can't time run backward?"

A friend once had an opportunity like this. He told me

of an encounter with Richard Nixon almost fifty years ago, when Nixon was running for president and his motorcade went through the small town near the college where my friend was an undergraduate. "I hated this man so much that I decided I wanted to hate him in person," he says. "So I got as close as I could, just to take a look. The motorcade stopped near where I was standing and Nixon started working the crowd and coming closer and closer to me. I desperately tried to think of something to say as he approached, and I came up with what I thought would be really vicious. He stuck out his hand, I refused to shake it, and I muttered, as bitterly as I could, 'How's Checkers, asshole?'" [Nixon's famous dog, Checkers, not Checkers's asshole.] "Nixon kept his ghastly smile plastered on his face and made his way over to the platform where he was to make a short speech. The first thing he said was, 'I just met a fine young college boy in the crowd and he was kind enough to ask how Checkers is. I'm happy to tell you all that Checkers is fine and is looking forward to living in the White House.'"

Prepared remarks may not often fare *this* badly in real conversation, but they do tend to fall flat or interfere with the natural flow of the occasion. In fact, the dinner host's (surely) rehearsed gibe did bring the table's conversation to a halt, as a home run often can bring to an abrupt end a dramatic and complex inning in baseball. Jokes, a terrible weakness of mine, have the same effect. If they're good, they are conversational culs-de-sac. If they're bad, they're culs-de-sac with mud puddles at the end. Most of us use reliable phrases and responses and small witticisms from time to time. I am embarrassed to admit that when someone asks me how I am, I often say, "Fine, given the human condition." The late Gardner Botsford, a wonderful *New Yorker* editor for many years, and much sunnier than I, always answered the same question, "Never better."

But that kind of canned ham, however self-caricaturing it becomes, doesn't impede conversation, unless it becomes the principal ingredient of the exchange—as it does with such parodic brilliance in Jonathan Swift's *Polite Conversation*. Some scholars and writers have taken this satire and its introduction by "Toby Litt" to be a real guide to witty repartee. I can't figure out why, when such passages as these inflate the lampoon so broadly:

COLONEL: This wine should be eaten, it is too good to be drunk.

LORD SMART: I'm very glad you like it; and pray don't spare it.

COLONEL: No, my lord; I'll never starve in a cook's shop.

LORD SMART: And pray, Sir John, what do you say to my wine?

SIR JOHN: I'll take another glass first; second thoughts are always best.

People frequently precook what they're going to say in order to be funny or witty, which, in keeping with matters electronic, raises the question of Googling new acquaintances before getting together with them. (Naturally, this matter has no bearing on accidental meetings.) The answer to that question depends on two factors: age and practicality. Age: Most people under forty or maybe forty-five Google new people almost by reflex. They crack the pixel-spine of Facebook or occupy MySpace as a matter of course. Older people, those who use phone books and Maxwell House coffee and reminisce about—well, just reminisce at all—tend not to. Practicality: If the conversation you're about to have has clear implications for pragmatic advantage or other practical consequences of any kind for you, no matter what your age, Google the person, I'm sad to say. If neither is the case, no matter what your age is, don't Google the person. Chances are you will know a little anyway, of course, but if you do a more thorough job of checking out, you will lose the possibility of the delight of the unexpected. Refusing to reconnoiter about the other person is like refusing to know much about a movie before seeing it (a kind of luxury these days, what with so much chatter about popular culture filling the bandwidths) or like traveling somewhere without consulting a guidebook beforehand.

If you offend someone by not knowing "who they are," it may well be a sign that it's not worth knowing who they are. A guy who found himself seated next to David Remnick, the editor of *The New Yorker,* at a fancy Manhattan dinner party not too long ago told me this story. After they introduced themselves, the guy—a very accomplished and important scientist—said to Mr. Remnick, "So, what do you do?" In literary New York, this is a little like going to dinner in Los Angeles, sitting next to Steven Spielberg, and asking what he "does." Or Omaha and Warren Buffett. Or London and Tom Stoppard. Or Nashville and Dolly Parton. But the guy told me that Remnick seemed relieved rather than insulted not to be recognized—a sign of character.

As a member of the Maxwell House generation, I'm told that Googling and Facebooking and MySpacing are standard operating procedures in

DATING...

AND COURTSHIP these days.

Lots of books and manuals offer everything from reasonable, if obvious, counsel about dating to advice that bristles with attitude and calculation, often in the service

of hooking up. At my stage of life and in view of the number of intelligent and/or angler's texts on this topic, I can't
really add much to this particular conversation. But I can
animadvert a little. But first, speaking of Googling, from
ArtOfSeductions.com, here's an example of the quality of
much of the dating advice offered by that vast, global teenagers' room* called the Internet:

> If you just arrived and accessed her in three sec-
> onds, she will know it was spontaneous because she
> noticed you arrived whether she wanted to or not—
> you were a change in a static environment. Or if
> she just arrived and you accessed her in three sec-
> onds, she will recognize the spontaneity of it again,
> because you couldn't have accessed her before—she
> simply had not yet arrived. If, however, you just pop
> out of nowhere—she didn't see you arrive, neither
> did she just arrive, and the only change in a static
> environment was you accessing her—you just might
> set off her stalker alarm.

Or at least her syntax alarm. To show the futility of
some efforts at gender neutrality, take a look at the difference between that page, saturated with oafish testosterone
as it is, and one of the first Google page results for the
search term "How to Pick Up Men":

★ Metaphor courtesy of Charles McGrath, in *The New York Times*.

Are you really, really sure
you want to pick up men?

Dating may inevitably fall victim to reflective stratagems and instinctive behavior. Or "behaviors," as the psychologists like to say. Preening, chest puffing, arm touching, feigned uninterest, feigned interest, non-accidental accidental encounters, arriving late, and so on: These may be unavoidable ploys, programmed by our fiendish genes, into our primate ancestors. But when things go well, such moves eventually give way to simple good conversations. So I wonder, Isn't it better—even when refraining from revealing too much too fast—to be oneself as much as possible from the beginning? This is a cliché, but clichés become clichés for a reason—they tend to be true. Writing this very sentence is a painful example of not putting off until tomorrow what I can do today. If someone is attracted to someone you are only pretending to be, the disparity will surface like Grendel and track both of you down later and hurt you. And the same goes if the person you're seeing wears personality camouflage. One of the most attractive moves anyone can make on a date is to fairly quickly and insofar as possible stop acting as if he or she is on a date. To cease performing under such circumstances takes confidence and a certain amount of serenity and acceptance about what may be a disappointing outcome. But trying to maintain the performance can have a far worse outcome, when the truth comes out later on. Listen to Samuel Johnson:

A youth and maiden meeting by chance, or brought together by artifice, exchange glances, reciprocate civilities, go home, and dream of one another. Having little to divert attention, or diversify thought, they find themselves uneasy when they are apart, and therefore conclude that they shall be happy together. They marry, and discover what nothing but voluntary blindness had before concealed; they wear out life in altercations, and charge nature with cruelty.

Before leaving this unfortunate youth and maiden to founder on the shores of marital misery or bob in mutual resentment in the bay of divorce court while their attorneys argue about whether the youth's baseball card collection is community property—before leaving behind the eternal and overconsidered dilemmas of dating and courtship and romance—a further word or two about ways of avoiding this predicament, besides the anodyne "Just be yourself, dear."

Back to seductions. The word *seduce* originally derives, perfectly enough, from the Latin *sub* ("below" or "under") and *ducere* ("to lead"). For a while in the sixteenth century, it denoted, nonsexually, a drawing away from proper service. If I or someone else seduced you in 1546, say, especially if you were someone else's vassal, it might mean only that I distracted you or led you astray from your duties.

The sexual—even unphysically sexual—meaning of the word fits perfectly under the general umbrella of leading astray or subversion of duties, for a seduction, in life and literature, usually entails not meeting one's emotional responsibilities, not only toward another person but toward oneself. There may be an element of seduction, mutual or one-sided, at the beginning of most relationships, but everyone has a duty to himself or herself and to others to keep in mind, however schizophrenically, the emotional damage that deceitful conversational dissembling can do.

Most important of all, in this particular conversation, is the heavy—onerous—duty one has to oneself. You cannot be seduced, in the rascally sense of the word, without your own complicity. To "I should have known," many psychologists and therapists would respond, often accurately, "You did know." This conscious or unconscious self-deception does not excuse the exploitative exploits of Casanovas, but it does show that our old provocateur/friend Socrates' dictum "Know thyself" has one of its chief apps in matters of the heart and conversations about and within those matters. You must not only hear but listen. And not only to the other person but to yourself.

This is not to say that dating must always be a freighted and solemn matter. Teasing in moderation is an essential ingredient of dating, an important test of resiliency and un-self-seriousness. "Rattle, rattle," a girl once said to me a long time ago, imitating the way the loose change and keys in my pockets announced my approach and celebrated my departure. "Okay, Sarge," I once said to someone else when she issued certain interesting orders. Teasing is like kicking the tires of a car before buying it or flicking the rim of a wineglass with your fingernail. If the connection between two people can't withstand a bit of ribbing, then it is certainly not going to withstand the real mettle-fatigue tests that are sure to come.

When teasing turns chronic or sarcastic, the implement becomes a weapon, sharp and dangerous. It's a sign that the other person doesn't like you or you don't like her or him. Or it may be a character trait, a reflexive habit, that precludes its possessor from ever achieving the kind of intimacy that survives and in fact often grows out of teasing. Moderation in all things (as Aristotle is said to have advised his fellow Athenians). Except, apparently, moderation.

Before we leave our couples to find or lose their ways, as couples have always done and always will do, a few remarks about matches that may or may not be made.

Courtship, and the conversations it involves, often feel crucial to their participants. And they certainly can prove to have been crucial. A marriage made, a passion consummated, a heart broken, a shotgun wedding required, a child born, a dynasty begun, an extended-family web woven. In this way, dating conversations resemble other possibly crucial-seeming conversations that have as their basis more immediate and concrete goals and agendas. I am referring here to job interviews, deal-making or deal-breaking business meetings, college-admissions interviews, and so on. They all potentially have to do with forming serious and sometimes even permanent connections.

Even though such conversations are far from aim-less, they deserve some consideration here, because adopting a certain, less intense perspective on them—a perspective borrowed like an umbrella in a rainstorm from non-goal-oriented encounters—can reduce the awful anxiety with which they are often approached and conducted. Please remember: A successful job interview (one that results in being hired) may be crucial. But it may also keep the applicant from getting a different job that would have been better. That is crucial, too. A successful merger discussion (one that results in, well, a merger) may be crucial. But it may keep one or both parties from other kinds of business opportunities later on. That is crucial, too. A successful college interview (one that ensures admission) may be crucial. But it may also deprive the applicant of the chance to be taught by Professor Lifechanger, at another institution. We just don't know what we may be missing if our proposal or application or deal is accepted, but we tend to narrativize what does happen to us as being what was meant to happen to us. Meant by what—or Whom—I would ask.

The fact is that unless we're just plain lucky or unlucky in love or in life, both randomness and character will more fully determine our fates than any particular plan or meeting or interview will. The economic and geographical circumstances of birth all by themselves are random—and often genuinely crucial. The daisy game of (s)he-loves-me, (s)he-loves-me-not is a wonderful floral embodiment of the arbitrariness that governs not only romantic fortunes but also much of the rest of our lives. But the way our minds work makes us ill-equipped to take into account such matters of luck. You understand these kinds of contingencies more clearly later in life, but if you can understand them earlier, that understanding may spare you a good deal of worry and its consequent pharmacy expenses.

Don't be blasé about these kinds of conversations. I'm not saying that. We can't help wanting what we want, and if we don't want to want anything, we can always become Zen monks. But try to draw some serenity from realizing that most do-or-die meetings turn out to have been more like do-or-wait-until-next-time meetings. And always try to take a genuine interest in the person you're talking to, irrespective of your own mission and goals. Within the limits imposed by the agenda you are both following, remember that you're to some extent trying to pass not only some kind of test but also the time of day.

When I applied to be a fact-checker at *The New Yorker,* I found myself dressed quite similarly to the man who was interviewing me. He was the magazine's executive editor, and his office was littered with racing forms glowing with yellow highlighting, evidently for betting purposes. We both had on charcoal-gray suits, which were the uniform of that day, and blue shirts, different blues but still, and red ties, different reds and patterns but still. He had on wingtip cordovan shoes and I had on plain cordovans. We talked. I had no particularly relevant experience, though I had been a teacher for a few years. But in those days a plain old BA would do for a job like that. But as I was leaving, and thinking it hadn't gone too well, I happened to glimpse my résumé on the man's desk. It was what he'd been using to take notes on, I realized. Across the top of it, in all capital letters, he had written "WELL-DRESSED!" I got the job.

Such discussions are generally not occasions for

KIDDING AROUND,

WHICH IS ANOTHER important part of lively social talk. A good, spontaneous sense of humor is, along with curiosity and "impudence," *essential* to good conversation. These three conversational components are so crucial that they deserve a chapter of their own, and they're just about to get it. In the meantime, some ne'er-do-well, or at least seldom-do-well, cousins of humor are here, looking for a handout of attention:

1. Sarcasm. A little goes a long way, as I've just said, though it can occasionally be a useful special tool, like a fishtail file in woodworking. Example: A linguist giving a speech remarks that double nega-

tives in sentences result in positives, as they do in mutliplication. But that, as in multiplication again, double positives never yield negatives. Whereupon someone in the audience shouts out sarcastically, "Yeah, yeah!" Sarcasm belongs mainly to youth— to the age of around twenty-five, when life begins to get serious for those for whom it has not become, sadly, much more serious much earlier. When people begin to clamber over the rocks of adult life, being made fun of naturally hurts more, because the need for self-respect and dignity increases. And even sarcasm not directed at another, but of an all-purpose nature, wears thin faster than New England pond ice in mid-April.

2. Class Clowning. A constant stream of jokes and mots extinguishes any chance of making conversational connections. I should know. At its most extreme, it can also be a sign of real trouble: Excessive punning and wisecracks often signal mental illness. I taught school once with a French teacher (from the actual country of France) whose wordplay in the faculty lounge got more and more frantic, until it became noticeably compulsive. He seemed obsessed with fooling around with his new language and would say things like "Meester Cook eez not such a good chef, eh?" and "Theez eez a school of dead feesh" more and more often. And then after a midyear break, the rest of the faculty was told that he had been institutionalized for schizophrenia, after a canoe trip during which he almost froze to death—which just goes to show that you can't have your kayak and heat it too. So very sorry, William Shawn.

Why William Shawn? Speaking of puns, William Shawn, the longtime editor of *The New Yorker*, hated them, an aboriginal distaste inherited from the magazine's founder, Harold Ross. I once wrote a "Talk of the Town" story during a transit strike about hitchhiking around Manhattan, which ended with a dialogue between me and a fellow pedestrian. I asked him how he was getting around, and he said, "Diesel." I said, "Diesel?" He pointed to his feet and said, "Diesel get me anywhere." Shawn cut that line and I tried to restore it before it went to press, when the piece was in galley proof. He called me into his office and said in his quiet voice, "Mr. Menaker, I understand you want to put back the original ending of your 'Talk' story." I said, "I know we usually don't use puns, but this one seemed pretty good." He smiled in pain and said, "I think you must not understand that to use this pun would *destroy the magazine*." He always ran that line in defense of *The New Yorker*'s increasing calcification. Discussing certain employee benefits would destroy the magazine. (He didn't exactly say that a dental insurance plan would destroy the magazine, but I was told that he did say, angrily, in a meeting of the short-lived Employees Committee, "Dostoevsky didn't have a dental plan!") Photographs would destroy the magazine. If a water cooler was moved even an inch, Shawn would probably have said that it would destroy the magazine. It was this very rigidity that almost destroyed the magazine, but that's another story, in psychologically direct conflict with the topics of

CHI

But wait! Chapter 5 isn't over. What was my response to the dinner party host's "Well, Dan, you *do* like to talk!" I think I tried to "forget" about this on purpose, because I'm afraid what I said was: "Why would you say something like that?" I couldn't help it. I just knew that he had been planning this sally all along. And *I* had just been listening to *him* hold forth for quite a while. He said, "Come on, Dan—Jim and I were just joking." I said, "It doesn't sound all that much like a joke to me." This made the silence of the table even louder. He said, "Oh, no— this is going to be one of those moments you hold on to a grudge about forever." So now I was a blowhard *and* a grievance nurser. A woman to the rescue, as is often the case when conversation repair is needed: The hostess said, "Dan, you know my husband admires you and is jealous." Perfect, even if possibly untrue and untrue, in that order.

Perfect, also, in its reflection of what Deborah Tannen calls women's tendency toward "rapport-talk" and men's (that is, in this episode, my) inclination to turn conversation into a contest, through "report-talk." Tannen's popular-sociology best seller *You Just Don't Understand: Women and Men in Conversation* discusses conversational gender differences in fascinating and plausible ways, so I will leave it to her, er, seminal work and that of other sociologists to bear most of the burden of the talking aspect of this eternally controversial Venus-Mars topic. You will have to read it personally, I'm afraid. But like the Dunbar/ Emler/Gazzaniga statistics about conversation cited in the first chapter, Tannen's thesis is open to debate, based on everyday exchanges. I said I wouldn't get into conversational gender distinctions, but I will, after all, back into them in order to get out of them quickly. Here are *my* specious and trivial gender difference observations, drawn on anecdotal evidence of the flimsiest kind from a severely limited demographic:

1. As already noted, women take longer to say good-bye than men do. Women would basically

have it go on forever, this valediction, which usually includes questionable assurances of getting together again very soon, usually "next [time unit here—weekend, week, month, spring, year, reunion]," and the loveliness of everything about the house or restaurant and cuisine and decor. Men just want to get away fast, fearing that they may yet manage to screw up the miracle of social civility that they've just accomplished.

2. At restaurants, women want to know what everyone is ordering. Men don't. Men regard their food orders as proprietary information. When asked, they may put that information up for sale at auction before the waiter takes the orders. Women examine menus as if they were the Dead Sea Café Scrolls, holding culinary secrets that have never before been revealed to a world that desperately needs them. Men regard menus as necessary inconveniences, to be dealt with as one deals with seat belts. Women will always wish they had ordered the thing that someone else ordered, while men would never admit to such a mistake and will choke down the crab cakes with vanilla beans and puree of ibuprofen without complaint or comment. Women will want to "try" others' food. Men find this very trying. When men order dessert, they tend to order dessert. Women, after repeating the required "I shouldn't" three times and ritually laughing at their own naughtiness, proceed to regard this part of the meal as a temptation of Faustian dimensions. But they will ultimately succumb to the waiter, who has had to circle back three times during the Agony, at which point he assures the martyr that the Caramel Cacao Delight with Chocolatey Chocolate über-Chocolate Fudge-Mud Drizzle Brulée is "beyond delicious— the Vatican just certified it as 'sinful.'" Finally, for women food is fabulous, amazing, or delicious and sometimes all three. Rarely, a little disappointing. For men it's good or not very good.

3. Women repeat themselves more often than men do. Rephrased repetitions are a kind of conversational grout for women or like free extras at the cosmetics counter. For men—except at business meetings, whose main feature for both sexes is often a requisite echoing of what others (especially bosses) have said—repetition is a felony. The trouble, for men, is that this frame of mind often leads to missing or failing to give or clarify important details that can be lodged inside repetitions like new boarders in an old house, which can in turn lead to being there at three-ten instead of ten to three and buying a ticket to Guinea rather than Guyana and not understanding that it was *Alice* who happened to see *Ben and Dorothy* stealthily checking into the airport hotel, not *Ben* who happened to see *Dorothy and Alice* stealthily, and so on.

4. Women are spatial in their conversation, while men are linear. Women knit the social fabric, men want to get to what they insist is the point.

5. Women, being naturally more polymorphous than men are, touch others more during conversation than men do.

6. There is *always* a sexual element, buried however deeply, in conversations between heterosexual and for all I know homosexual men and women.

It's time to stop the silliness, which is what most premises like Tannen's are. Or, at least, a good conversation between a man and a woman—between any two people or among a group of people—soon turns such grossly valid generalizations into nonsense, as it will with regional or racial or religious or generational generalizations. Yes, maybe there's an element of truth in them. But such data seem to me to hold water in order for it to be boiled away by the huge number of exceptions that take place in most of our lives every day. One of the purposes of a really good conversation is to supersede theories and statistics about conversations. The human habit of apparently aim-less talk may have started with physical grooming, but it has become what in some ways is its opposite: a meeting of the minds.

Now, for real, on to

CHAPTER 6: CHI

NOT THE VITAL ENERGY that, according to certain Asian philosophies, flows through all matter—the "*chi*" that concludes "*tai*." But, conversationally speaking, something like it: an acronym for the three vital components of good conversation: curiosity, humor, and impudence. Duh! you may be thinking with regard to the first two, if you possess these qualities and if you are impudent to boot. Just "Obviously" if you are non-impudent. And yes, the first two items do on the surface resemble something like archetypes of "Duh!" But they also have often noticed but seldom articulated subtleties and complexities, an understanding of which I believe will illuminate and foster good conversation. The third vital energy of talk, impudence, seems less immediately essential and may even strike you as antagonistic to the courtesy that conversation calls for. But a slight twist of its derivation, from the Latin for "without shame," comes closer to the way I mean to use it here. It has more to do with a playful, childlike mischievousness and uncensoredness than with giving offense. And when it's used carefully, it functions as a kind of marvelous social equalizer—it unstuffs shirts. But first:

CURIOSITY

AT *The New Yorker,* a long time ago, a vivid Irishwoman named Maeve Brennan—better known in her era as the "Long-Winded Lady," who gave voluble reports to the magazine's then anonymous or pseudonymous "Talk of the Town" pages—went mad. She had been teetering at the edge of total derangement for a long time, and she finally tumbled into it fully. She turned into a haint, walking the halls of the magazine with her vermilion hair and smeary lipstick as if permanently affronted and in search of restitution for ancient grievances. One day she threw a pint carton of milk against the glass panel in the door of one of the magazine's editors. It exploded and made a mess of the window and the door and the floor below.

A craggy, workmanlike journalist who was just barely on the eccentric side of craziness himself—always approaching the real point of his writing but landing just to the side of it—came into my office right after the milk bomb incident. "Did you hear about Maeve?" he asked in his customary doomsday tone. He shook his head solemnly. "Yes, I did," I said. "It's very sad." The writer sat there in deep reflection, as if pondering man's or at least Maeve's fate. At last he said, "I wonder where she got the milk."

Yes, laugh. I almost did right then and there, but it wouldn't have seemed polite, in the face of the journalist's solemn inquisitiveness, however odd its angle. This incident at once parodies and underlines what may be the sine qua non quality of mind of a good conversationalist: curiosity (which carries along with it attentiveness—that is, listening). If you don't have a genuine interest in the world around you and in others, no matter how entertaining you are as a storyteller, you will in the long run be at best a performer, at worst a bore.

In an exaggerated way, the off-kilterness of the journalist's question points up a certain *kind* of curiosity that serves any conversationalist well but that the self-help guides seldom bring out into the open. Nothing wrong with straight-ahead, obvious questions: "When are you due?" "How was O'Hare this morning?" "Really—from a thrift shop?" But it's the curiosity that surprises the other person, and sometimes even oneself, that brings the most interesting answers. Journalists know this. By instinct or training, they attend closely to the cracks and corners of what their subjects say, because they know that the shadows there often hold the most interesting information.

An example: Once, before live-camera real-time images of the local weather were routinely used as part of local weather forecasts, and before any forecasters were certified meteorologists, I was writing a couch-point-of-view piece about three weathermen in New York. I noticed that every now and then what they said was or wasn't going on outside at the moment wasn't or was. How could that be? I was just curious—it was a kind of marvel. So I asked to interview the three guys in person and on the job, and it turned out that none of them had windows to look out of. That is the truth. Following forward from this discrepancy between report and reality, I got curious once again about whether people ever acted on their frustration about inaccurate TV weather. One of my subjects, who had a sense of humor about his work, told me that a viewer had recently sent him what he (the viewer) called a "weather rock." It was an ordinary small rock with a string around it. "Hang it out the window," the viewer instructed. "That way, if it's wet, you'll know it's raining, if it's dry, you'll know it's not, and if it's swinging back and forth a lot, you'll know it's windy." He went on to suggest that the weatherman might thereby improve the accuracy of his descriptions of "current conditions." As often happens in journalism, some of the best stuff—in this case "lite" but sometimes very serious—comes from reporters bringing questions from the back of their minds to the front.

A nonjournalistic and more aimless example: A friend of mine was once talking to someone older whom he had just met and became curious when the older person happened to mention completely in passing that he had gone to a Quaker college and had taught at a Quaker high school. About to say good-bye, they were discussing "thee"-ing and "thou"-ing, because at the end of an evening, one of the older guy's uncles, a Quaker, would always tell his guests, "Thee may stay or thee may go, but don't ooze!" The younger man asked which school, the older man told him, and it turned out that they had been there—teacher and student—together, decades earlier, for one year and knew dozens of people in common. A truly serendipitous Discovery, and the basis for a stronger connection.

So when you're talking to someone, for the sake of his or her and your own interest and engagement, listen very closely not only to the loud notes, but to the quiet ones and grace ones as well—to what sounds as though it's being downplayed or skipped over. Such attention is, for one thing, flattering, but it also yields insights that the people we're talking to sometimes don't even know they have. A wonderful young *New Yorker* writer stopped by my office once and we exchanged pleasantries. Then I asked him what he was working on, and he said, "Oh, not much right now. I have a 'Talk of the Town' story in the magazine next week, but it's no big deal—you know, just a little nothing. Like a thousand words or something." This protest sounded very much like too much to me. I had read the story in galleys and admired it, and since I know all too well and shamelessly share the desire for approval that all writers have, I was curious, and a little concerned, about this almost clinical self-effacement. I said, "It didn't read like it was just dashed off. How long did it take?" He said, "Well, thanks. It took two whole days—and the night in between." I said, "Then it *is* a big deal. It's really good, and it's in *The New Yorker,* for God's sake." He hesitated for a moment, as if thinking the exchange over, and then said, "Plus two days of reporting, which I didn't mention. You're right—I worked very hard on it. . . . I make a habit of running down my own work, and I think I ought to stop." We both smiled smiles of confessional recognition of a goal we shared: recognition.

That incident and the recorded conversation between Fred and Ginger exemplify the often confessional nature of the risk taking that good conversations always contain. Another exemplification: In an aim-lessly congenial lunch, a lawyer who specializes in intellectual property involving serious literary matters mentioned to me the long car commute he has to take to get to his work in Boston. Okay, I thought, a version of spare time. I have a sort of obsessive curiosity about others' spare time, as I myself have so little of it and when I do have it turn it to so little use. "So, do you listen to the radio or CDs—or just audiobooks, for your work?" "All of that," he said. "But mostly music," he added. "What music?" I asked, hope beginning to dawn in my ashamed heart, as it always does, almost always to no avail, when this subject comes up. "Oh, everything," he said. "Classical and jazz—you know, all different kinds of music." The flame of hope flickered. "Right," I said. "Well, it's nice to have that time as long as you're not stuck in that awful Boston traffic." He looked down at his plate and mumbled, "And mmph." "Say again?" He looked up and stuck out his chin a little. "Country—country music," he said with an edge of defiance. Well, I love country music, and this passion has brought me no end of embarrassment and ridicule among allegedly sophisticated friends and family. So though there was no ice to be broken at this lunch, the conversational water suddenly became much warmer—and funnier, as in:

HUMOR

IN THIS INSTANCE, it took the form of narratives about the contempt in which our surprisingly shared enthusiasm is generally held by those close to us. "My son calls it 'Murrikin music,'" I said. "He hates it. Everyone thinks I say I like it in order to be provocative. This has gone on so long that by now, that's probably true."

The lawyer told me that a potential client of his had heard Toby Keith playing in the background when he called the lawyer at home and on that musical account decided not to retain his services. I *love* Toby Keith and have even gotten my son to respect him. I told of having lunch with a powerful magazine executive who out of nowhere informed me that his sister was a country singer. This man is known for risky conversational surprises—about strife in his childhood, about serious motorcycle injuries narrated in a "nothing unusual" fashion, about firing people, about family matters, such as: I asked him once—I'm reverting here to the rewards of curiosity—about the wooden necklace he wore, the man-necklace that I now realize launched at least one man-bracelet: mine. He told me, "Well, you know, after I got a divorce, I went through the obligatory affair with a younger woman, and she gave me a necklace, and I wore it. After I met my second wife and we got married, I kept wearing that same necklace for some reason. It bothered my wife. One night when I was in bed, she came into the bedroom with nothing on and a pair of scissors in her hand." I swear to you that without immediately realizing what I was doing, I crossed my legs at this point in the story. "She came over to me, leaned over the bed, and snipped the old necklace off, and gave me a new one, and this is it."

Back to country music. "What kind of country music does your sister play?" I asked.

The guy said, "She had a number one hit!" (To write good dialogue, as the old rule goes, never have what any character says respond directly to what another character has just said.)

I said, "Number one hit! Amazing! I probably know it."

He laughed and said, "I don't think so."

"Why not?"

"It was a number one hit in Japan—that's why."

Then, after he explained the puzzling Japaneseness of his sister's career, and since he had previously mentioned the obligatory affair with a younger woman precisely in such an offhand way, I asked him about that, and he told me more.

No one has ever really written well about what makes any remark or any person or any story funny. Exhibits A–C:

A.

What Is Humor?
by Steven M. Sultanoff, PhD

The answer to that question is not a simple one.

First, humor is the experience of incongruity. In one's environment the incongruity may be experienced when someone falls down in a situation when they are not expected to fall down, or the incongruity can be between concepts, thoughts, or ideas often illustrated by the punch line of a joke or the caption of a cartoon.

—From the Association for Applied and Therapeutic Humor

B.

What is the purpose of humor? Why do we laugh? Humor is a complex phenomenon. There is no general theory of humor or even an agreed definition. When we try to define exactly what counts as humor and what does not, or how humor operates, we find it quite difficult.

—Dr. Chaya Ostrower

C.

> Humour or humor is the tendency of particular cognitive experiences to provoke laughter and provide amusement. Many theories exist about what humour is and what social function it serves.
>
> —*Wikipedia*

Even Freud's essay "Jokes and Their Relation to the Unconscious," brilliant though it is, ultimately suffers the fate of all serious writing about humor. It holds that jokes and much of humor in general owe their pleasures to the infantile gratification of the superego, allowing the ego to acknowledge primitive, unconscious . . . Never mind. Writing intellectually about humor is like writing about the taste of food by molecular analysis. Still, I can theorize with the worst of them, and I will say that at least in conversational terms, and I think in general human terms, all humor derives from the Great Joke. The Great Joke is the condition of our existence. I mean, here we are, with the ability to figure out a lot of things, more and more things every day, amazing things, maybe even stuff that happened before the universe was created—in other words, things that happened before anything happened, for Pete's sake, things about soil-moisture ratios and wolverine mating habits and Picasso's influences and the connection between primate grooming and human conversation and the provenance of antique armoires and— But we haven't the faintest clue as to *why* we're here. The imams, rabbis, priests, and ministers can claim that they do, but sorry, guys, you just don't.

As with all of us in our descent from Mitochondrial Eve, every joke, funny remark, slapstick performance, and irony descends from the Great Joke. The nucleus of every funny atom is the Great Joke. Before I tell you why this matters in conversations—even serious ones, *especially* serious ones—I need to first tell you the most incisive if not the funniest joke I've ever heard—a joke that, like most jokes, consists of a conversation.

Two missionaries are captured and tied up by an isolated savage native tribe in a vermin-ridden village in a benighted land. The chief says to them, "You have choice—death or *moogli*." Yes, he speaks English. Pretty amazing. One of the missionaries figures he would rather live to spread his spiritual message no matter what *moogli* might be, so he says, "I choose *moogli*," whereupon the tribe proceeds to beat, abuse, and ridicule him. They urinate and defecate on him, torment him physically in every way, and leave him a shattered man. The chief turns to the other missionary and says, "You have choice—death or *moogli*." The other missionary, having seen what *moogli* is, decides that the God he serves would prefer him to choose death. "I choose death," he says with brave defiance. "All right, death," the chief says. "But first—*moogli*!"

Well, this is the very definition of unfairness: a microcosm of the unfairness of being given the powers of choice and consciousness but entirely foiled in our effort to understand the meaning of our simple existence. In other words, the Great Joke. You can understand everything, except, wait! You can't understand the main thing you want to understand. This plight—a radical *cluelessness*—underlies all humor, and its implicit recognition plays a crucial role in conversation. That is, cluelessness is embedded in modesty, so crucial in establishing close connections between people. Modesty contains a grain of the Great Joke.

This is why an element of self-deprecating humor works well in conversation. An extremely respected and successful friend once said to me, "Every time I try to type, 'I'm afraid,' it comes out, 'I'm afraud.'" Humor about distant events or people works, too, as long as it's not too derogatory—the story about the exploding milk carton may be an example. Or the anecdote about William Shawn on Dostoevsky's dental insurance status. Good humor in conversation always says, on some level: We are all ridiculous. When we tell a story that makes someone else seem silly and dumb, we should and usually do tell it in a way that signals our own fellow-foolishness. But as we've seen, sarcasm, except among people (particularly young men) who know one another well and have issued one another a wisecrack pass, generally falls flat exactly because it posits the opposite of the Great Joke. It says that the sarcasmer may believe that he isn't in the same boat of bafflement everyone else is in. Isn't, on an important level, the "poor, bare, fork'd animal" of Lear's famous self-pity moor party.

People can't "learn" a good sense of humor, unfortunately. Those few who don't have one make friends, marry, and hang out with others who don't. The solemn marry the solemn, and if they don't, they're in trouble. But most skeletons do include a funny bone *somewhere*.

Sarcasm is a close cousin of

IMPUDENCE

WHEN BACKGAMMON WAS A FAD, just after the Pleistocene, I wrote a magazine piece about it. A professional gambler was the champion then. Well, of course he was a professional gambler. He and maybe twenty or thirty others like him made a round of tournaments whose first prizes were six figures. As I recall, the top prize for this tournament— one of the biggest, held in New York—was $250,000. I interviewed this guy a few times, once in a very fancy, gilt-furniture, gilt-mirror New York hotel suite. He was proverbially tall, dark, and handsome and was wearing a gold-colored robe closed with not so much a belt as a *sash*. He was affable but unrevealing—wouldn't talk about his winnings, cheaters, mind games. He stuck with backgammon strategy and a wrinkle-free version of his life story. In the middle of the interview, a beautiful, dark-haired woman walked out of the suite's bedroom, wearing similarly boudoirish attire. The man looked very much the gambler, the woman very much the gambler's moll. But that (no rings on their matrimonial fingers) was as racy as things got. The interview was fine, "fine" often being one of the most damning words in our language.

I wasn't getting what I needed—at least a glimpse of or a quote about the darker side of the pro gambler's world. My deadline was approaching like the walls of a car crusher—my side-view mirror had just snapped off. I went downstairs in the hotel and desperately sought out another top player, this one in the ballroom where the tournament was being held. He had just won his match and was sitting to the side, looking quite the aristocrat: gray three-piece suit, neat white hair swept back from a smooth, noble dome, pearl cuff links, a vaguely English accent, like that of American movie actors in the thirties. He was similarly close to the vest, the original cliché for a gambler. I tried to sidle up to questions about controversies, rule breaking, angry confrontations, and, again, winnings. No (so to speak) dice. Finally, in exasperation and as not so much a Hail Mary as a Farewell Mary, I asked a question that I knew was out of bounds for most gamblers. I said, "What's the most money you've ever bet on a single game of backgammon?"

"What? I can't believe you asked that question."

"I thought I would give it a try. At this point, unlike everyone else in this room, I have nothing to lose."

"Well, you've got a nerve, I must say," he said with a slight smile. "What impudence!" He turned away from me.

I guess I'll have to try to make a meal of the pabulum I have, I said to myself.

Douglas Fairbanks turned back to me. "But I will tell you this," he said with a distant gleam in his eye. "It was for more money than is at stake in this entire tournament."

"One game?" I said.

"One game, young man," he said.

"Did you win?"

"Of course I won," he said. And then, impudently, "Do you think I'd mention it if I hadn't?"

And then he told me much more, on the condition of his remaining anonymous and unidentifiable, though the description of him here is as accurate as memory allows.

Impudence, as I define it here, has less to do with shamelessness, its Latin-derived meaning, than with conversational nerve—one of the words the gambler used. It has to do with speaking up with what you want to say but are afraid might be taken amiss. It has to be governed very carefully, and it is not welcome in serious business transactions—as I should know, since, along with other traits, it probably led to my final decision to de-corporatize. When he hired me, one of my bosses said, "I've heard you're more of a wise guy than I am. You'd better watch that." (Although wise guy–ism—I prefer "wisdom guy"—served me well at least once, when in one of my hundreds of editorial meetings in publishing a very young editorial assistant mentioned a "top secret" book proposal from a third-rate agent, all show and no shame, who had said on the phone, "Wait, I have to close my door so my assistant won't hear what I'm about to tell you." Forgetting the self-censorship that I had developed, however spottily and imperfectly, I said, "Right—except there was no door and no assistant." That got a big laugh, eased the tension in the room, and was the end of this editorial blind alley.)

You have to have nerve and the confidence of that nerve to be really good in conversation. You have to be pure of heart—that is, you have to know that the nervy remarks you make and the questions you ask proceed from a kind of momentarily restored childlike frankness and inquisitiveness rather than adult snoopiness or prurience. As Hume said back in the eighteenth century (and back in the second chapter), "Nothing carries a man through the world like a true genuine natural impudence." And you have to be able to judge well the person you're talking to, in terms of playfulness and resilience. When I was interviewing the brilliant singer/songwriter Neko Case, she was describing the small Vermont town she was moving to, leaving Tucson. I mentioned a book of photographs I'd seen about hunters in Vermont's North Country—heavy men with beards and rifles, surrounded by mounted antlers in their hunting lodges.

"I love beards," she said. "Muttonchops are the best."

I said, impudently, "Well, sorry, but that means you have to love Ulysses S. Grant."

She said with surprising passion, "Ulysses S. Grant was the *hottest!*" I had my quote but pushed on.

"But he was so portly," I said. "I don't see the two of you together."

"Portly is *really* hot, too."

The best opportunity for using impudence effectively is the dropped handkerchief—

—which bears a close resemblance to those quiet asides that invite curiosity. People drop handkerchiefs in conversation all the time, even if they aren't aware that they do and don't expect them to be picked up and returned, with a wink. You can always break down formality—your own and that of the people you talk to—with a well-chosen bit of nerve. If someone says to you after a long exchange, "My husband and I disagree about this," you have probably been invited to impudize something like "And nothing else—amazing!" If someone says to you in the middle of a narrative, "But for once I had slept very well the night before . . . ," you can pick it up later and say, "Do you know how annoying that bit about sleeping so well was?"

Young people are especially reluctant to be curious *or* mischievous with older people, and for the most part this respectfulness suits them well. But not always. I've found that older, well-set, conservative types often enjoy being surprised by a little impudence and unexpected questions from younger people. It allows them to come down from the perch of convention where they usually have to sit. On the other hand, impudence can of course end a connection with an elder or a superior instead of continuing or deepening it.

CHAPTER SEVEN

AFTER WORDS

———— ⌣ ————

Contemporary journalism and the Internet have re-
duced the plain English form of a perfectly respectable brain chemical, oxytocin, from "the trust hormone" to
"the love hormone" to "the cuddle hormone." "The cuddle
hormone." Well, not here. Here, it is and will remain oxytocin, derived directly from the Greek *oxytokion*, medicine
speeding childbirth. And that, among many other things,
is what oxytocin—a neurotransmitter secreted in both
men and women by the pituitary gland—does. But since
childbirth is not one of the occasions normally associated

with much besides rudimentary and in fact often subverbal communications, oxytocin's other effects are more pertinent here. Well, actually, not all of them, because we also secrete oxytocin under other minimally verbal or subverbal circumstances—when we (I mean, you) breast-feed and when we have orgasms.

Except that the intense bonding involved in breast-feeding and sex do actually bear indirectly, but closely, on oxytocin's relevance to conversation. For just as those two primal functions (and, amazingly, a simple touch alone; so a handshake not only shows that we are unarmed, but also pokes your pituitary) raise the level of this chemical, so does—voilà!—conversation. I mean, if you sit down with someone and have a good talk, your sense of well-being afterward has not only a conscious component, but a neurochemical one as well. The one proceeds from the other. It is a "high" and one that, like other highs, is habit-forming, but usually in a good way. You want more of it. You want more of it especially with those who are "good" at it—which means that these others release in you that physiological reaction of feeling better, feeling good.

Why only "usually" in a good way? Because we all know conversation junkies, people who allow their hunger for talking to others to become so intense as to interfere with other aspects of their lives. To say nothing of our lives, when we're on their hook. They grow so habituated that the benefits of conversation erode, and the people turn into bores—not only to others but even to themselves. You can often see (or hear) in their own ennui what maintaining their habit costs them. A few Christmases ago, I went to a party where I ran into a writer whom I'd worked with on one novel a few years before that. He talked so much during the lunches and editing sessions we'd had throughout the publishing process that even though the book was reasonably successful, I purposely made an offer for his next book that was too low for him to accept. I couldn't go through those conversational ordeals again. And sure enough, age had not revived nor custom freshened his infinite blather. It's not that he just talked and didn't listen—he did listen. But the whole encounter still seemed to be an automatic one, with listening and questions intended not as a way to reach any conclusion or understanding or fellowship, but as a way of keeping the dirigible of talk airborne for its own blimpy sake. And this time, I thought I could actually see a kind of desperation in his eyes—like Linda Blair's stomach in *The Exorcist,* on which, in welts, the normal little girl wrote "help me" from within her demon-occupied body. "Shut me up," the guy's welts would have said.

Even more of us know even more others whose lack of conversational ability and avoidance of social interactions we refer to as "withdrawal"—another interesting coincidence with drug vocabulary. Such people often seem (and are) depressed. But we shouldn't conflate the laconic with the anomic. Some few of the best conversationalists are the least wordy. For example: At *The New Yorker* once, I got in a scrape with my alleged superiors for writing a piece for another publication about unsolicited short-story submissions. I took one such story and in the middle of the essay used it as the basis of a pastiche of bad writing. Given *The New Yorker*'s smug and secretive and publicity-shy ways, I can only ask: What was I thinking? And answer: Obviously not much. I disguised the prose thoroughly, so that its author could not prove that he had been held up to public ridicule. But he did recognize that his writing had been used for satiric purposes, and he wrote an angry letter to me and *The New Yorker*'s management, threatening to sue. *The New Yorker*'s lawyer, Milton Greenstein, who famously advised his colleagues not to buy Manhattan co-op apartments because they could never work financially, called me on the linoleum and bawled me out. I was yet again in trouble, which had come close to being not my middle but my first name at the magazine.

I figured I'd better consult a lawyer about the possibility of being sued and/or fired, and I did. A friend recommended the late Charles Rembar, who was a famous First Amendment lawyer, but I didn't know that. He, as the attorney for the Grove Press, is the reason you can buy and read D. H. Lawrence's *Lady Chatterley's Lover* and Henry Miller's *Tropic of Cancer,* among many other, far filthier texts, without fear of being arrested. Now, for all I know, Rembar was a yakker at other times, but in the one legal

consultation we had and at a subsequent lunch, he was extremely succinct and concise in his conversation. He also
realized that I was poor; maybe that accounts for the brevity of the business meeting. I remember that at one point I
asked whether *The New Yorker could* fire me for my breach of
their etiquette. He was silent for fifteen seconds or so, and I
said, "Because in strictly legal terms, I don't know—"

He raised a couple of fingers to me to indicate that I
should be quiet. He then said, "I am actually *thinking*." He
actually thought for what seemed like another minute and
then said, "No." So much had gone into that "no" that I
felt as if we'd had a conversation without having had one.
He paused for another thirty seconds or so and said, "But
they can always find another 'reason.'"

"Well, I think I should write an apology to Greenstein," I said.

He thought for another minute. Then he said, "That is
masochistic. You have done nothing wrong or illegal."

"But they don't like this kind of thing."

Another long pause. "That's their problem. If they take
action against you for this, and if they say that's the case,
then they are in more trouble than you are. They know
that." Another pause. "And anyway, nothing should be in
writing from you that doesn't have to be in writing."

We sat there silently for a few minutes. He seemed to
be actually ruminating more than thinking. "May I see the
piece again—and the story?"

I gave him both. He read them silently for a few minutes. He smiled broadly. "You idiot," he said. Then, "This is very funny." Pause. "You don't have a contract with *The New Yorker* which might specify against your doing this sort of thing, do you?"

"No."

Another pause for reflection. "Why do you think you wrote this?"

"Despair over having to read the slush pile," I said.

"Well, that's only one of the reasons. Writers like to show off. They want attention."

I took some seconds of my own and pulled myself together and said, with some impudence, "And lawyers don't?"

He laughed. "Oh, we do, but most of us learn pretty quickly to keep the ball inbounds."

We sat there for a full two minutes. He finally said, "I will write a letter for you to Mr. Greenstein and to this guy." Another pause. "Nothing will happen to you at this point, I would say."

Some days after the letter was written and sent, Rembar asked me to lunch, and we had an excellent, succinct time. Both occasions gave me that mild high and sense of well-being which a good talk almost always produces. The oxytocin effect, no doubt. We didn't become fast friends, but at least for my part, I felt we'd made a strong connection, even though—no, *because*—he was such a thoughtful and verbally economical man. As the philosopher E. M. Cioran says, "Silence in the middle of a conversation suddenly brings us back to essentials."

When people are depressed, on the other hand, a paucity of words manifests psychological isolation rather than thoughtfulness. Think of such types as Max von Sydows and the others—the Rembaresque people—as Gary Coopers. A good friend or a sympathetic acquaintance or a good therapist will try to draw out the von Sydows conversationally. If it doesn't work, the depression is probably clinical, and some neurochemical Ingmar Bergman is directing their lives. When it does work, the lifting of spirits must in some way result from a physiological change in the brain. Even when some difficult objective circumstance cannot be changed, conversation about it may change the way we regard it. It's as though we have somehow managed to mix in part of another person's more positive or compassionate nature—his inner Tom Hanks or Reese Witherspoon— with our own inner von Sydow. As though that other person has pushed the button in our pituitary gland that releases the trust hormone into our higher brains.

For decades now, a famous French obstetrician, Michel Odent, has done research into the role that this neurotransmitter, oxytocin, plays in human childbirth and development. Odent was among the first to revive the use of birthing pools for women in labor, pioneered the use of intimate, private birthing rooms, and introduced the "gate" theory of labor pain and lumbar anesthesia. Dr. Odent may be a little *fou* when, in a book called *The Scientification of Love,* he proposes that because for such a long time human survival depended on competition and aggression, we deliberately if unconsciously interrupted the natural and private process of childbirth by having it in "clinical" places, with strangers and machines present. (Like everything else, the book's title sounds so much suaver in French: *L'amour scientifié.*)

In any case, Odent believes that a widespread return to a more "natural" and private childbirth whenever it's medically possible may actually change society as a whole away from its present competitive ways to gentler, more cooperative, and trusting ones. Whether or not this idea makes any sense, what does make sense—what our daily experience confirms—is that satisfying, non-goal-driven conversation enhances our lives and makes us feel good. And that this benefit results from neurobiological processes in our brains. And that these processes involve oxytocin. And if modern childbirth methods or any other anthropological practices generally result in a failure to turn on the trust switch, then maybe we can jiggle it into functioning later on by talking to one another.

If our activities don't release oxytocin internally, apparently oxytocin applied from the outside can release our activities. One of many diverse reports about this phenomenon appeared in the periodical *Biological Psychiatry* in March 2007. The experiment's premise was the common observation that understanding what others are thinking and feeling—reading their minds, in a way—is crucial to successful personal interactions. Basically, conversations. In their double-blind, placebo-controlled experiment, scientists took thirty male human volunteers, sprayed the thirty nostrils of fifteen of them with oxytocin, and administered to all thirty the famous "reading the mind in the eyes" test, in which the subject looks at photographs of thirty-five sets of eyes and chooses one of four descriptions of the emotion in and behind those eyes ("angry," "reflective," "confused," and "suspicious" might be offered for one photograph). Those who got the oxytocin did markedly better on the test. The report concluded that the effect "was pronounced for difficult compared with easy items." I scored 23 out of 36—just barely in the normal range. If you could see *my* eyes right now, you'd have no trouble detecting some embarrassment, since I am writing this book about good social interactions. My daughter, one of the sweetest and most observant people I know, got 32. Here is the Web site: http://www.glennrowe.net/BaronCohen/Faces/EyesTest.aspx.

Among this substance's other miracles: When injected into a male rat's cerebrospinal fluid, oxytocin produces instant erections; oxytocin evidently accounts for sexual fidelity in the prairie vole, one of the few mammals besides us that practices monogamy, or at least says it does; virgin female sheep show maternal behavior toward lambs not theirs (obviously, them being virgins and all) after being injected with oxytocin; oxytocin may reduce repetitive behaviors in autistic children; in various psychological tests, including one called "the ultimatum game"—in which a sum of money is given to two players, the first of whom decides how to split the money and the second of whom can accept or reject the offer, but by rejecting the offer denies money to both participants—a spritz of oxytocin appears to heighten altruistic behavior. Essentially, this means the first player tends to offer a more generous split.

With specific regard to conversation, oxytocin's effect on children and adults with autism, a condition that interferes with both communication and the ability to "get" the feelings of others, seems most significant. In 2007, *American Chronicle* published a piece about this hormone by Susan Kuchinskas, a journalist who runs an entire Web site about oxytocin, hugthemonkey.com. The piece reports on experiments by Dr. Eric Hollander that started about five years ago, in which oxytocin was given to autistic patients and two important improvements took place: Repetitive behaviors diminished, and, once again, many individuals did much better at recognizing the emotional states of other people. In other words, they *saw* them more clearly as other people. Logically speaking, seeing others as others required them to see *themselves* as others in the eyes of others. This is in essence the central weight-bearing beam of conversation.

Don't think that pharmaceutical companies haven't tried—with great energy and enterprise—to capitalize on oxytocin's powers. One of many, many examples:

Learn More About Liquid Trust

IMAGINE
- Getting whatever you ask for
- People trust what you tell them
- Having a competitive edge over others

These things are possible. The key is oxytocin. When people trust you, doors are opened that were always closed before. . . .

Liquid Trust gives you the added edge by releasing oxytocin into the air around you. When you walk into the room, almost immediately people will have a different feeling about you. Their oxytocin level is rapidly rising. Throughout the day, Liquid Trust is working for you.

Whether it really works or not, the idea of bottled or sprayed trust used as a tool for social or commercial success conflicts directly with the very nature of trust. Also, I'm wondering if "wearing" oxytocin wouldn't compel the wearers themselves to *be* trustworthy—unless they're wearing face masks or something like that, which would be a giveaway that something strange was up—and tell whoever their business or sexual or social targets were not to trust them because they were wearing Liquid Trust. But, then, that would make the targets trust them, so you end up with a sort of social Möbius band of trust and nontrust. (Did you happen to notice the Baron Cohen name in that Web address about the eye test? To add another paradox to this situation, the "reading the mind in the eyes" test was invented by Simon Baron-Cohen, first cousin to Sacha Baron Cohen, who plays the entirely untrustworthy prankster Borat.) Better to let nature take its course or maybe hurry it along by oxytocin-rich childbirth, having a lot of sex, and having a lot of conversations. The bonobo ideal—if for "a lot of conversations" you substitute "grooming and even more sex."

Even if we can't pacify or monogamize the entire human population by internal or external chemical boosters—if our reptilian lower brains figure out a way to turn the peace and kindness into profit and hookups and eventually more death and destruction through the use of fiendish oxytocin atomizers like Liquid Trust—we can enrich and elevate our individual lives by understanding the great rewards of good conversations, deliberately seeking them out, getting better at them. You don't need to be a neurobiologist or know anything about oxytocin to have these rewards. Human consciousness, an utterly unique and I believe forever inexplicable phenomenon, confers upon us not only the blessing of intelligence, but the curse of loneliness. That is, we alone as a species are *aware* that we are walled up inside our own minds, cut off from others by the very fact that we *are* aware. A bacterium or a barn owl may be able to *be* sad or happy, but you can bet that it doesn't *know* that it is. One of the few ways to climb that wall, or speak through a chink in it, is to talk together.

Although conversation is a reciprocally generous behavior, it ultimately serves the self, as the experiments with autistic people show in a clinical setting. Not in the narrow sense, selfishly, but in a much broader one. In finding out who the person we're talking to is—what his or her complaints and complexities are, his or her tastes and toxins, his or her angels and demons—we find out who we are, especially if he or she returns the courtesy of attention and has the curiosity and humor, and impudence, to draw us out. In knowing others and allowing ourselves to be known, we know ourselves.

"But you said that this sort of conversational dowsing can be of *pragmatic* use. How so?" you might ask. Well, as we've seen, by talking to someone else, drawing someone else out and having yourself drawn out, you can often discover what's on the deeper levels of your mind. You may not realize how concerned you've been about financial matters until you look back on a conversation and grasp consciously that dollars kept rearing their little wiggy George Washington heads. Or that a story you told about your kids—or your parents!—contained a profound kind of pride that you hadn't previously had direct access to. Or that the trip to the Yucatán wasn't entirely the gastroenteritic nightmare you'd been thinking it was. In fact, travel conversations frequently bring out retroactive pleasure that may have gone unrecognized in the face of flight delays, small, dark hotel rooms, incomprehensible tour guides.

So what good does this kind of understanding do you? You can *act* on it, if you're able and so inclined. You can address your financial anxieties more directly, you can tell your kids how proud you are of them, and you can overcome some of your resistance to travel based on its minor logistical and digestive setbacks. Like everything else worthwhile, these efforts are just that—efforts. Work. I recall reading somewhere (many places, actually) when I was much younger that relationships require work. This seemed to me not fair. You worked all day and then went home and had to work some more? Even dreams are work, according to Freud; he coined the word *Traumwerk*. And being a good conversationalist and enjoying conversation's benefits also take work, the lazy child in me is still sorry to say. But you are paid handsomely for this particular occupation. And this is precisely what good therapy accomplishes: insight followed by action.

Remember that amateur theory about humor in conversation and how all humor derives from the Great Joke of our very existence? Well, there is an amateur corollary, an expansion of that idea, that probably belongs here. It is this: Most good conversations seem to me to address—sometimes way below the surface, sometimes floating right on top, like a fly in the ointment of existence—the Great Insecurity. That is, like the conversation in chapters 3 and 4 between Fred and Ginger, most conversations, one way or another, involve admissions of our feelings of inadequacy, our mistakes, the partial fraudulence involved in acting like an adult when we know that we often still feel very much like children. If we don't admit to our weaknesses, we put ourselves in danger of losing our strengths.

These reflections are the meat and potatoes of psycho-therapy and analysis, and of true friendship—of making existential and even pragmatic use of this self-knowledge. If you will just let your mind and memory muse and reflect a little, you will, like a dowser, almost always find a deep theme or two running like an underground river below the whole encounter. This is what I tried to demonstrate by looking at the Fred and Ginger conversation. All really good conversations include, overtly or silently, the mutual under-standing that our lives are mysterious and often difficult, and that that is why we turn to each other and talk to each other: so as not to be alone in the difficulties and the mystery.

————

THINKING ABOUT CONVERSATIONS you've had can prove useful in two ways. One way is figuring out what makes you yourself tick and then possibly winding or rewinding or unwinding yourself. The other is far more woo-woo and embraces no less than—humanity in its entirety! Since a good conversation always involves finding common ground, it means that differences will have to retire to the sidelines, at least for a time. We live in an era when it's not just a good idea to try to get along, but—with the apocalyptic weaponry we have developed and the environmental havoc we are wreaking on our planet and the ever smaller world of the Internet age— imperative. Barack Obama ran an important part of his campaign on the premise and promise of talking to people with whom we have differences. It *is* kind of hard to punch someone in the stomach or fire an RPG at him or burn his house down while you're talking to him. In *The New York Times* last year, the Israeli filmmaker Ari Folman, who produced and directed the award-winning animated movie *Waltz with Bashir*—about his experiences during the war in Lebanon and the massacre at Shatila—had the following, ultra-pithy exchange with interviewer Deborah Solomon:

Q: Do you find that talk is . . . effective in war and diplomacy?

A: Yes . . . Talk, don't shoot. Talk.

There is one war that can't be avoided, and that's the war within our own natures between aggression and territoriality, on the one hand, and compassion and empathy, on the other. This is Dr. Odent's war—and a conflict that many other scientists and philosophers and statesmen have come to understand is the most important one being fought right now. For my part, I fear that our better natures are going to lose. I fear that the ancient evolutionary commands of individual and tribal survival and genetic propagation will not give way broadly or quickly enough—if they ever could—to more co-operative motives and instincts. Too much stands in the way, a large part of that "much" being religious fanaticism, abetted often by extreme nationalism and dire poverty.

It's tempting to deplore not just religious fanaticism but religion as a whole, as Christopher Hitchens has done with such power and eloquence in his book *God Is Not Great*. Because, as we've seen, most ordinary people agree that religion has a conversational cordon around it, even thicker than the one that surrounds politics, with signs saying, "Do Not Enter," for people who don't know one another well. The reason is that the subject is beyond reason. You can't really talk about something that by definition is irrational. That would be fine, if only there were more evenhandedness, a confinement as well as an exclusion, in this conversational taboo. That is, if you must worship this God or that God, no one should be allowed to encroach on your right to do so; but, correspondingly, you must never use your faith in the service of political or social purposes.

Far better would be to admit religion into the open arena of conversation. I believe if we did that—if we were bold enough about it—even religious people would eventually have to concede that either we will learn to get along together and achieve common goals on our own, without the help of any divinity, or humankind will perish. The faithful can retroactively attribute progress in these areas to a god-head or a godelbow or whatever, but the victory over our more combative instincts, which now serve us so badly after millennia of serviceably seeing to our survival and increase, will come from our own heads, our own hearts. Our own actions will determine our future, and for a good future, prominent if not preeminent among those actions must be talking to one another—conversation.

Now, Stephen Miller, author of *Conversation: A History of a Declining Art,* and Catherine Blyth, author of last year's *The Art of Conversation,* deplore what they see as a general deterioration in conversation because of the impact of such communication distractions as e-mail and texting and cell phones. Blyth:

> The irony of this communications age is that we communicate less meaningfully. Not despite but because of our dizzying means of being in touch. . . . Communication tools may bring us to-gether, but equally they keep us apart.

Miller:

> Neither digital music players nor computers were invented to help people avoid conversation, but they have that effect.

These two citations contain hidden fireworks of meaning, which I will set off for you right now. The "keeping apart" part of the Blyth diagnosis applies not only to electronic devices but to the original device that created them—laissez-faire capitalism. Yes, I know: Where did that come from? Hold on—you'll see, I hope. And the "weren't invented to help people avoid conversation" slice of the Miller covers the *purposelessness,* the blind plunging ahead, that drives human inventiveness. We have come up with the technological means to map our own genome, to destroy everyone, to create babies in all manner of surrogate and cloning ways, to give us lettuce that will be unaffected by temperatures from absolute zero to Fahrenheit 452 and that will play a Beethoven string quartet or "Peggy Sue" as it is picked, and, soon, to give us much, much longer, if not eternal, lives. As ethicists throughout the world have said, starting back when the atomic bomb was made, we have reached the point in our scientific development where it isn't just a good idea but apocalyptically crucial for us to impose moral and social control over the forces we've unleashed with our minds before those forces control—and destroy—us.

Like capitalism, technology tends to become a sort of Being, a blind, thoughtless entity that has its own way of taking over our lives, like cancer in an individual person's body. Capitalism drives communications technology in two ways: in the profits that are made from it—iPods! weapons! pharmaceuticals!—and in the tendency of these products *to make us work harder and longer.* A corporation is a Legal Person, don't forget, but when left unregulated and unsupervised, it is ultimately a sociopathic Legal Person, a tyrant. It tears families apart, dehumanizes those who serve it, and permits only the lowest possible wages for most of its minions.

Money may talk, but it doesn't want *us* to. Or at least, not about anything but it. Going way back to the business conversation of chapter 1, in which I wondered idly about what a book depository is only to incur my colleague's sharp rebuke for not sticking to business, I would say that it wasn't really her doing the talking. She was just the Linda Blair through whom the Great Satan of Gain was speaking. We cannot go on serving these demons of our own devising. If we don't rein in these marvels-turned-menaces, and if we don't manage to make communal and cooperative motives and sustainable goals supersede the impossible grails of endless growth and ever greater profits, and if we don't tear down or at least sequester the empty, virtual Babel that our society threatens to become, we're finished.

Conversation, itself ancient, is an active antagonist to these other, now more dangerous ancient drives. It takes time and energy away from them and offers its own, far richer rewards and satisfactions, once the basic necessities of our existence are met. It also creates in-person connections among people as opposed to virtual contacts and thus builds, brick by brick, a *real* human and humane community. "Brick by brick" is important; conversations of the kind I'm advocating here bear a strong metaphorical resemblance to the local-food movement and individual and community ecological reform and grassroots politics. I mean, it really does come down to one person at a time. Well, in conversations, two or three or four people at a time. Large social changes grow out of individual transformations, not the other way around. As I've said, I don't think we're going to manage this huge shift from individual competition and unregulated capitalism to global community, but of course I hope I'm wrong. It doesn't mean we shouldn't try. It means we should.

In my own, no doubt cockeyed way, I actually believe that our most recent presidential election represented an unconscious mass recognition of the necessity to shift social and political and individual gears. And surely that vote was at least partly a repudiation of the truculent, anticonversational, macho-man anachronism of the previous administration, which one hopes was the last gasp of radical Hemingway/John Wayne–ism in the United States. Judging by President Obama's demeanor, I would be surprised if he didn't allow—hasn't welcomed—digressions and curiosity and humor, and even impudence, from time to time. "Yeah, I'm left-handed," he said while signing an executive order during his first days in office, and then he added, "Get used to it." And, after all, this is a man who famously said of his marijuana use, "Yes, I inhaled. That was the point."

By the time you read this sentence, we'll have had some time to find out whether the president has maintained this demeanor of openness and to see if the nation really is, in its politics and foreign policy, turning away from confrontation to conversation. I do subscribe to the maxim about the greater decibel level of actions over words, and I don't think that as individuals or a people we can let down our guard in a hostile world. But I hope, against what I see as the odds, that more of our most important actions will actually *consist of* words.

The trouble is, as I said a few paragraphs ago, being able to enjoy the rewards and benefits of conversation can happen only "once the basic necessities of our existence are met." For millions if not billions of human beings, that condition is horrendously far from satisfied, and the poverty and over-population and exploitation that so oppress so many multitudes breed the anger, violence, and fanaticism that keep us from reasoning—even getting—together in a global way. If it's also the case that large social changes, the kinds of changes that might actually ensure the basic necessities of existence, depend on individual transformations, then it's up to our leaders to foster and enable those transformations, as, in modern times, Gandhi and Martin Luther King Jr. have done, and, in ancient times, Jesus tried to do. But as a worldwide enterprise, that is an extremely tall and probably unfillable order, politics and the thirst for power being what they are.

Still, we must do what we can do. With Hume, I believe that every time people talk together in a social and mutually gratifying way, the world becomes a better place. I also believe that despite the evanescence that is part of their very definition, some good conversations linger, like Keats's "unheard melodies," like the memory of sunlight after dark.

Because they happened, they are happening still. You may see a good painting or hear a piece of music only one time, but that one time is all time.

Outside of members of my own family, I was lucky enough to have two great teachers in my life. One was Samuel Hynes, an English professor of mine in college and an accomplished memoirist who taught me about the poetry that continues to this day to say for me what I can't say for myself, consoles me in tough times, and resolves emotional and logical conflicts with the touch of a metaphor. See Mr. Keats's "unheard melodies" in the previous paragraph. The other was the late William Maxwell, an editor and a great American writer whose work is right now undergoing a welcome rediscovery and who helped me become an editor at *The New Yorker*.

The evening of the day that the results of the honors exams at college were posted, Mr. Hynes (as he will always be to me, even though he long ago asked me to call him Sam) invited me and a friend for celebratory drinks. "My boys!" he said when he opened the door, and he proceeded to help us get good and drunk. I slept that night on the couch in his library. When I got up, with one of the first hangovers and maybe the worst hangover of my life, he handed me a glass of orange juice and said, memorably if nauseatingly, "This will cut the phlegm." We sat down for a while and talked about everything, including many of the subjects that parsing *The Waste Land* during seminar hadn't left time for, and I left feeling more exhilarated by our conversation than by the good results of the exam. That conversation lives with me and always will. Mr. Hynes and his wisdom about life and language live in these very words, and he knows how grateful I am to him, because I've told him.

That morning lives with me as does a conversation I had with Mr. Maxwell (as he will always be to me, even though he asked me long ago to call him Bill) when he lay dying. I had the impudence to tell him how much I resented his leaving me at *The New Yorker* at the mercy of people who didn't like me, without much in the way of warning or advice. I thought that would make him laugh, to be chastised jokingly on his way out the door of life, and it did. He chuckled and then said, quite seriously, "I knew you'd be all right." I replied, "I'm glad someone knew that, because I sure didn't." And he laughed again, and then I thanked him for everything he had done for me. Dying has to be done alone, I've learned, but given enough physical comfort, good company can ease that loneliness.

Both of these conversations were in different ways valedictory, and they seem appropriate for the ending of a book. They both demonstrate the lasting effect that good conversations can have despite their transient nature. They also show that like other human artifacts of physically more durable natures, some conversations, which are the most civil aspect of our civilization, endure, in their own way, far beyond our own lives.

HIGHLY SELECTIVE
BIBLIOGRAPHY

Stephen Miller's *Conversation: History of a Dying Art* (New Haven: Yale University Press, 2006) was an invaluable if occasionally dolorous resource for historical information about conversation.

Conversations of Socrates (New York: Penguin Classics, 1990), by Xenophon, edited and translated by Robert Waterfield and Hugh Tredennick, is not only essential but often amusing reading, especially the part where the Athenian interlocutors talk about how people should smell. *The Collected Dialogues of Plato: Including the Letters*, edited by Edith Hamilton and Huntington Cairns, translated by Lane Cooper (Princeton, NJ: Princeton University Press, 2005), has many words to live by, of course, including, from *Crito*, "Then, my friend, we must not regard what the many say of us: but what he, the . . . man who has understanding of just and unjust, will say, and what the truth will say." In the introduction to *De Officiis*, by Cicero, translated by Walter Miller (London: Macmillan, 1913), we're reminded that Cicero wrote the work in the form of a letter to his son, Marcus, who was twenty-one at the time, studying at the Peripatetic school of Cratippus in Athens, and, according to the translator, "sowing what promised to be an abundant crop of wild oats."

Closer to the present, we have Baldessare Castiglione's *The Courtier* (1528) and Giovanni Della Casa's "Galateo" (1558). At one point, the former, in the translation by Thomas Hoby 450 years ago, tells us that besides being adept at mannerly conversation, the courtier must be able "To swimme well. To leape well. To renn well. To vaute well. To wrastle well. To cast the stone well. To cast the barr well." A lot to ask of your average courtier. A hand-scrawled note to the Google-scanned copy of Robert Peterson's 1576 translation of Della Casa's *Galateo* says "It bee sew woordey & repeateth of itsel that it dew ye boore." Maybe, but speaking of boredom, the part about yawning is very funny. And speaking of courtiers, *The Duel in Early Modern England: Civility, Politeness, and Honour,* by Markku

Peltonen, published by the Cambridge University Press in 2006, argues—beautifully, I think—not only that early courtly behavior in conversation was a sibling to courtesy in dueling but that both were fathered by the invention of the printing press. That is, the rules of both could be set down and widely disseminated.

Bryant Lillywhite, who wrote *London Coffee Houses* (London: Allen & Unwin, 1963), also did a book called *London Signs*, a heavy item (around eight hundred pages), which proves that the name of a pub called Bag o'Nails derived not from "Bacchanals," as urban legend would wishfully have it, but from the building's formerly having been home to an ironmonger's shop. In 1791, James Boswell published *The Life of Samuel Johnson*, which is so weary of finding itself in bibliographies that I'll let it sleep through this one. If you don't know Hume's essays—*Essays Moral, Political, and Literary*, first published in 1791—try searching for them online and then see if you don't want to read them all in book form. They admirably follow the advice that Hume himself gives us about writing and speaking—that "we ought to be more on our guard against the excess of refinement than that of simplicity."

I wouldn't recommend any of Denis Diderot's writings, partly because evidently very little of what he wrote concerns conversation directly, partly because I have read so few of them, and partly because, according to a contemporary, "All accounts agree that Diderot was seen at his best in conversation. He who only knows Diderot in his writings does not know him at all. When he grew animated in talk, and allowed his thoughts to flow in all their abundance, then he became truly ravishing." On the other *main*, Montaigne's great essays, particularly "On the Art of Conversation," as translated by Charles Cotton and edited by William Hazlitt, in 1877, make it often seem as though one of the most eloquent people who ever lived were speaking directly to the reader and hoping to be disagreed with, so that the conversation would continue. As he says, he prefers "that which pricks, rouses, and incites" to "that which tickles."

Peter Gibian's *Oliver Wendell Holmes and the Culture of Conversation* (Cambridge: Cambridge University Press, 2001) weighs in heavily and often psychoanalytically about, well, Oliver Wendell Holmes and the culture of conversation. This surprising and synthesizing book creates a kind of panorama of intellectual and social life in mid-nineteenth-century America, focusing on New England, and it elucidates what Holmes calls "house-breaking" in conversation, as opposed to "house-keeping." The former was Holmes's balance, consisting importantly of interruption, to the latter, which was, as he saw it, Americans' habit of keeping to themselves. In a way, Holmes was part of a social movement to redress the grievances of Charles Dickens and Fanny Trollope about American manners. Dickens, in *American Notes* (1842), writes about the company he had on a riverboat:

There is no conversation, no laughter, no cheerfulness, no sociality, except in spitting; and that is done in silent fellowship round the stove, when the meal is over. Every man sits down, dull and languid; swallows his fare as if breakfasts, dinners, and suppers, were necessities of nature never to be coupled with recreation or enjoyment; and having bolted his food in a gloomy silence, bolts himself, in the same state. But for these animal observances, you might suppose the whole male portion of the company to be the melancholy ghosts of departed book-keepers, who had fallen dead at the desk: such is their weary air of business and calculation. Undertakers on duty would be sprightly beside them; and a collation of funeral-baked meats, in comparison with these meals, would be a sparkling festivity.

Trollope (in *Domestic Manners of the Americans*, 1832): "There is no charm, no grace, in their conversation. . . . I have very seldom heard a sentence elegantly turned. . . . There is always something that jars the feelings or shocks the taste."

Robin Dunbar's *Grooming, Gossip, and the Evolution of Language* (Cambridge, MA: Harvard University Press, 1998) presents the most plausible theory of the development of language that I've ever read. I've read only one other, as I recall, but unlike Dunbar's seemingly bulletproof argument, it didn't reckon with the role that our ancestors' need for ripe fruit played in linguistic evolution. Michael Gazzaniga's *Human: The Science Behind What Makes Us Unique* (Ecco Press, 2008) has many wonderful passages about language and conversation. It magically makes you feel at once like an organism hugely and magnificently different from any other and also like just so much wetware.

Emily Post's *Etiquette in Society, in Business, in Politics and at Home* (New York: Funk & Wagnalls, 1922), for all its archaisms, builds a sturdy and distinctly American bridge between Victorian manners and this nation's pre-depression ebullience, commerce, and sophistication. "The joy of joys," she tells us, in her wonderfully energetic style, "is the person of light but unmalicious humor. If you know anyone who is . . . beguiling and amusing, you will, if you are wise, do everything you can to make him prefer your house and your table to any other; for where he is, the successful party is also."

In the here and now, you will find real urbanity and erudition wearing entertainment's raiments in a very good and recent practical-advice book about conversation— Catherine Blyth's *The Art of Conversation: A Guided Tour of a Neglected Pleasure* (New York: Gotham, 2009; yikes— *uncomfortably* recent!). Blyth is a Brit, and she snaps out her guidance with great (if sometimes brittle) wit. About greetings: "Respecting native customs is the first sign you can give someone that he should respect you."

Written dialogue is generally to conversation as a painting is to a palette, but still the great playwrights, screenwriters, and novelists have put before us exchanges that in a distilled and highly shaped way illuminate essential ingredients of everyday talk. Very arbitrarily, and without going into obvious detail, I would pick out from the rest: The often grouchy or at least querulous Choruses in classic Greek drama. Shakespeare, of course, especially *Hamlet*, which features one of the most egregious conversational buffoons of all, Polonius; and *Henry IV*, with Falstaff, not only witty in himself but "the cause of wit in others." Beckett, the genius of bafflement. Twain, for conferring dignity upon our humblest vernacular. And, in modern American fiction, Richard Price and Elmore Leonard, who practice the art of direct conversational indirection seemingly without effort.

It's easy to see why Dickens had such high conversational standards, as he discerned precisely so many speech habits and eccentricities and therefore was a great writer of dialogue himself. I'm not sure I've ever enjoyed any conversations more than the ones that Sarah Gamp, the nurse who is fond of her porter (the alcohol, that is), has with her doubly nonexistent friend Mrs. Harris, in *Martin Chuzzlewit*—a fiction within a fiction. She says in praise of herself but displacing, with obvious guile, that praise onto the meta-fictional Mrs. Harris,

"Telling the truth then, ma'am," says Mrs. Harris, "and shaming him as shall be nameless betwixt you and me, never did I think till I know'd you, as any woman could sick-nurse and monthly likeways, on the little that you takes to drink." "Mrs. Harris," I says to her, "none on us knows what we can do till we tries; and wunst, when me and Gamp kept 'ouse, I thought so too. But now," I says, "my half a pint of porter fully satisfies; perwisin', Mrs. Harris, that it is brought reg'lar, and draw'd mild. Whether I sicks or monthlies, ma'am, I hope I does my duty, but I am but a poor woman, and I earns my living hard; therefore I do require it, which I makes confession, to be brought reg'lar and draw'd mild."

Finally, if you are reading these words in a bookstore and are about to put the book down and instead buy *The Tearful Summer of Our Hot Forsaken Love*, by Lachryma Duct, don't. I've read it. It sucks. But if you must, then you will find in the print version of *The Economist* of December 19, 2006, under the headline "Chattering Classes," as succinct and sane a digest of the topic of conversation as I've ever seen anywhere. Too bad I can't find a byline for the piece. I'd like to talk to the author.

ACKNOWLEDGMENTS

Thanks to:

Jonathan Karp and my wife, Katherine Bouton, for their astute, prophylactic, and suspiciously similar editorial suggestions, and to Jon also for his prodigious publishing expertise and his composure.

Jamie Raab, for her blessing on this project.

Esther Newberg, my agent and irreverent good friend, for representing the book and then saying, "Now you have to write it."

Cary Goldstein, Harvey-Jane Kowal, Colin Shepherd,

and everyone else at Twelve for their advice and forbearance.

Sona Vogel, for the meticulous copy-edit.

"Ginger" and her predecessor test subjects Samantha Henig, Robin Henig, Arthur Phillips, Matt Pearson, Andrew Proctor, Ben Arthur, and Julie Klam.

Jacob Bronstein, for technical audio help, tact, and patience.

Ben Sonnenberg and Dorothy Gallagher, for making me part of countless wonderful conversations within the circle of their otherwise brilliant and funny friends.

Minna Fyer, for her wisdom and rich laughter.

Will Menaker, for his stalwart permissions work.

And the late Frederick Engels Menaker, my uncle, who wrote a book called *The Life of the Party* and always was.

ABOUT THE AUTHOR

DANIEL MENAKER is the author of two books of short stories—two of which won O Henry Prizes; *The Worst*, a book of humor (with Charles McGrath), which the Library of Congress has, bafflingly, failed to include in its catalogue; and a novel, *The Treatment*, a *New York Times* Notable Book, which was made into an independent film starring Chris Eigeman, Famke Janssen, and Ian Holm. He has written journalism, essays, and comic pieces for many prominent American magazines and newspapers, including *The New Yorker, The New York Times, Harper's, The Atlantic*, and *Country Music*. He was an editor at *The New Yorker* for twenty years and later became executive editor in chief of the Random House Publishing Group, where he worked with such distinguished writers as Billy Collins, Elizabeth Strout, Nassim Nicholas Taleb, Gary Shteyngart, and Sister Helen Prejean. He has also taught graduate writing courses at UCLA and the City University of New York, and was the editorial producer and presenter for the online book program Titlepage (titlepage.tv). He lives in New York City.

ABOUT TWELVE

TWELVE was established in August 2005 with the objective of publishing no more than one book per month. We strive to publish the singular book, by authors who have a unique perspective and compelling authority. Works that explain our culture; that illuminate, inspire, provoke, and entertain. We seek to establish communities of conversation surrounding our books. Talented authors deserve attention not only from publishers, but from readers as well. To sell the book is only the beginning of our mission. To build avid audiences of readers who are enriched by these works—that is our ultimate purpose.

For more information about forthcoming TWELVE books, please go to www. TwelveBooks.com.